ROSALYND

RYBURN RENAISSANCE TEXTS AND STUDIES

THOMAS LODGE
ROSALYND

Edited by Brian Nellist

with the assistance of

Simône Batin

RYBURN PUBLISHING
KEELE UNIVERSITY PRESS

First published in 1995
by Ryburn Publishing
an imprint of Keele University Press
Keele University, Staffordshire, England

© the contributors and KUP

Composed by
Keele University Press
and printed by Hartnolls
in Bodmin, England

ISBN 1 85331 106 5

Contents

Introduction

Most readers are not going to find Elizabethan prose fiction immediately attractive. There is a glassy regularity in its mode of expression which seems to render instantly unreal the situations it addresses. The imperturbable balance of its sentences seems even to threaten that flexibility of formulation which we associate with thinking, as though the rigid piling-up of antitheses and parallels replaces the actual operation of mind it is imitating, unlike the compression afforded by the couplet to eighteenth-century poetry. Yet in the contemporary verse the perfection of the form, in the sonnet for example, becomes the register of a potential detachment within the convolutions of emotion, which gives the reader the sense of powerful intelligence simultaneously within and outside the situations being embodied. Why then does it not happen this way in the prose narratives – with notable exceptions, say parts of *Arcadia* or Nashe's *Unfortunate Traveller*? Their popularity with a reading public that was also buying Shakespeare and Sidney and Montaigne is undeniable: *Rosalynd* went through eleven printings between its first publication in 1590 and 1642.[1]

We have to understand a distinct aesthetic in fact rather than simply try imaginatively to make up for a deficiency. The situations in the narratives are often extreme, strange, deeply involved in contradictions of ethic, Lodge's story not least. The dilemmas of feeling are continually distanced by the manner of narration, yet preserved in the substance of the writing. Moral assumption is left more ambiguous, without the guiding comment of the writer, to a much greater extent than in, say, *Rasselas* or *Silas Marner*. Johnson and George Eliot are also writing with a sense of the

---

1. Our text is a modern-spelling edition of the first quarto (Q1) of 1590, which was extremely well printed. A handful of obvious misprints have been silently corrected. There are a few minor variants in the edition of 1592 (Q2): those we have adopted are recorded in our notes; for a full list, see the textual notes to the edition of W. W. Greg, *Lodge's 'Rosalynde', being the Original of Shakespeare's 'As You Like It'* (London, 1907).

problematic in conduct, but are confident of their capacity to appeal to principles of judgement which the reader can be led to share. This is partly a matter of cultural difference. In the Elizabethan stories the reader is left with more to do and the assumptions seem more ambiguous. The writing offers instead a formal clarity and balance against the grain of the story.

The first character that Lodge creates is the author himself through his dedication to Henry Carey, Lord Hunsdon, where, ignoring his time as would-be professional writer, he presents himself as going straight from university to military service, a scholar and soldier, like another Sidney. The book becomes the expression of the soldier's delight in action and the scholar's interest in argument and eloquence. We should not seek in it accurate description or interest in strange places, and Bordeaux, the French court, the forest of Arden, remain simply names. The exotic finds entry instead in the Euphuistic array of legendary lore from the encyclopaedias, classical allusion, Latin tags and a French poem. The story exists rather to produce a series of situations that prompt the characters into oratory. They speak, often to themselves, to give shape to the problems in which they find themselves – the dying father justifying the preferential legacy left to his youngest son, Saladyn wondering whether to obey the will, Rosalynd finding she is falling in love with the unknown Rosader, Adam Spencer in the forest reflecting on the mischances of life and so on. If it sounds like a succession of dramatised essays where idea takes precedence over action, we should also notice that, characteristically, the self-addressed speeches lead back into specific action. Even the passages of conversation, as between Rosalynd and Alinda in the forest, are driven by a verbal combativeness. Because Alinda mocks Montanus' passion for Phoebe, when they first discover the poems pinned to the trees, Rosalynd, disguised as the page, feels bound to defend the male point of view. When Alinda replies, playing up to her role of *grande dame*, with a threat to whip him/her with nettles if she continues in that vein, the violence of the apparently light exchange disconcerts us, as the substance of the tale often does. The interest in eloquence is often sustained by tensions and contradictions, between individual desire and conventional solidarity. Montanus, for all his charming lyrics, becomes partly a figure of derision because of the uniformity of his stance as despairing lover.

In rendering so much of the story as speech, Lodge is departing greatly from his source, the fourteenth-century poem *Gamelyn* (though we do not know if there was some, now lost, intermediary text). *Gamelyn* was not printed in either of the big sixteenth-century editions of Chaucer, Thynne or Speght, which, because they included so many false attributions, became in effect anthologies of late medieval poetry. Even now, however, it appears in no fewer than twenty-six manuscripts of *The Canterbury Tales*, so Chaucer probably intended to rework it as a tale for the Yeoman. Sixteenth-century reading habits did not make the firm distinction between script and print that we do today, so, even without some lost secondary source, there is no need to imagine a Lodge involved in unlikely research into medieval archives for new material.

Gamelyn is not a courtly poem; it is written in couplets with a variable pattern of stresses and mid-line pauses, but its rough metric suits its material. Unlike *Rosalynd*, it is set in the England of the smaller gentry and tells of the three sons of Sir John of Bounds, John, Ote and Gamelyn, how the father's legacy favours the youngest son and how he is then defrauded by big brother John. The narratives are too close in detail for the relation to be merely a matter of two works telling the same story. When, for example, the youngest son first rebels against his treatment by his elder sibling, the poem presents the encounter as follows:

Afterward cam his brother	walkinge thare
And saide to Gamelyn,	'Is our mete yare?'
Tho wrathed him Gamelyn	and swor by Goddes book,
'Thou shalt go bake thiself;	I will nought be thy cook!'[2]

In *Rosalynd* this becomes

> In came Saladyn with his men, and seeing his brother in a brown study, and to forget his wonted reverence, thought to shake him out of his dumps thus: 'Sirrah,' quoth he, 'What is your heart on your halfpenny, or are you saying a dirge for your father's soul? What, is my dinner ready?' At this question Rosader, turning his head askance, and bending his brows as if anger had there ploughed the furrows of her wrath, with his eyes full of fire, he made this reply: 'Dost thou ask me, Saladyn, for thy cates? Ask some of thy churls who are fit for such an office …'

Lodge renders the ignominy of the question more exquisite – 'your father' but 'my dinner' – and he is interested in motive and intention to a greater degree, but the situation is the same. The *Gamelyn* poet uses the verbal exchange as a means of getting to the action as fast as possible, where Lodge brings to the shape of the narrative the concern of Renaissance rhetoric in the oralising of feeling and its expression in gesture. Abraham Fraunce, for example, would have recognised the causes of Rosader's response here:

---

2. *Middle English Romances*, ed. D. B. Sands (Exeter, 1986), p. 159.

The countenance must turn with the body, unless we cast aside the face in token of detestation or abhorring any abominable thing … The chiefest force of the head is in the countenance, and of the countenance in the eyes, which express livelily even any conceit or passion of the mind.[3]

The story of Rosader is essentially that of Gamelyn. The elder brother keeps coming to terms because of his sibling's sheer physical strength. Gamelyn goes to contend with a wrestler at a local festival, arrives just as he kills the two sons of a franklin, defeats and dispatches him, but, when he returns in triumph with his supporters, finds he has to break his way into his brother's hall which has been closed against him. He again subdues John into toleration, but is then captured and tied to a pillar in the hall where he is mocked by his brother's guests. The old seneschal, Adam the Spencer (steward), has secretly released him the night before, however, and he wreaks havoc among the company and occupies the castle. His brother, now sheriff, returns with a legal posse and Gamelyn and Adam have to break out of the hall and flee to the greenwood, where they join a party of feasting outlaws. It is at this point that the two stories diverge. Gamelyn in time becomes leader of the outlaws. His brother offers fair trial and the second brother, Ote, stands surety for him, but the judge has been suborned and the jury packed and Ote is in danger of his life when Gamelyn returns, assaults the courtroom and kills the traitorous John. The king, who is now involved, forgives Gamelyn and makes him judge over all his forests.

The differences with *Rosalynd* are important. For the provincial medieval poem, the king is a distant figure, a semi-divine providence who can read the events accurately and can recognise in the dispossessor John the true outlaw, the man who has corrupted the majesty of justice. If the social circumstances of *Rosalynd* are grander, the result is also to destabilise its figure of royalty. The wrestling match changes from a local contest, for example, into a courtly tournament arranged to divert the discontented subjects of a usurper. The bribing of a judge, a complaint also in other outlaw writing such as the Robin Hood ballads, is transformed here into the negotiation of Saladyn with the wrestler that he should kill Rosader, where in *Gamelyn* John can only pray that his brother should not return from the match.

Gamelyn seems to have been written with a specific audience in mind. Like the Robin Hood poems, it is written for an audience of retainers in hall.[4] It glorifies younger sons, the victims of primogenitive inheritance.

---

3. *The Arcadian Rhetorike* (London, [1558]), sigs. J8v–K1r.
4. J. C. Holt, *Robin Hood* (London, 1981), pp. 71ff.

The heroic father, despite advice, insists on leaving the major inheritance to the son most like himself. The older ways of reward for prowess and personal achievement are vindicated against the newer ways of the law, which becomes in effect a conspiracy between tricksters and the rich, often clerics, to hang onto their gains. *Gamelyn*, like the Robin Hood stories, is notably anti-clerical. The combination of social rank, knightly family, and lack of social position, no wars in which cadets could win prizes, status or land, produces a cult of the rebellious, the outlaw, who is a protest against this sense of grievance. The dream is that the king himself speaks for a nobler law which will do justice by the younger son. *Gamelyn* is a notably tough poem, with an interest in the details of rowdy conflicts in the hall and a very rough sense of justice. It has no female characters at all.

Yet if *Rosalynd* is in ambition a more courtly tale and replaces the ruffian of the poem by the princess of the title, the effect, in changed circumstances, is somewhat similar; reward becomes not killing your elder brother but marrying a rich, titled lady and making your way to the top by a good alliance. Sexual attraction has political status in Lodge's story. As the daughter of the banished king Gerismond, Rosalynd has no place in the court and Torismond fears that her beauty will automatically inspire some ambitious courtier to win back the kingdom on her behalf. Love is not simply a personal feeling in this tale; it is a political threat. In the medieval poem the king can raise an outlaw to be a judge; in the Renaissance fiction the king himself is an outlaw and the *de facto* sovereign manipulates the law to his own advantage. The troubles of the last years of Henry III and the difficulties of the Bourbon succession may lie somewhere behind a story which has been, after all, relocated in France. For all its distancing rhetoric, *Rosalynd* acutely dissects the ways of *real-politik* and its adjustments to ideas of justice. When Rosader is driven into the forest, it is the usurper who supports his rights and throws Saladyn into prison, though only in order to gain his estates. The bad king, for the worst of reasons, delivers a perfect judgement: 'by thy means have I lost a most brave and resolute chevalier. Therefore, in justice to punish thee, I spare thy life for thy father's sake.' The father's legacy again ensures that Saladyn is punished simply with banishment. In *Gamelyn* the corrupt administration of the royal law could be attacked in the name of the king himself. In *Rosalynd* the malpractice goes all the way to the top, yet the wrong motives produce here the right judgement. Torismond is a master of Renaissance statecraft. The authority of fear is veiled by public splendour, as when he appears at the wrestling tournament:

> accompanied with the twelve peers of France, who, rather for fear than love, graced him with the show of their dutiful favours. To feed their

eyes, and to make the beholders pleased with the sight of most rare and glistering objects, he had appointed his own daughter Alinda to be there, and the fair Rosalynd, daughter to Gerismond.

'Feeding the eyes' is what lovers do, but these are political 'appointments' not the commands of Cupid. We are first of all told that the peers attend specifically not out of love, and are then offered a description couched in terms of love, where court ladies become the expensive gewgaws of royal display, 'rare and glistering objects'. The irony is that, in consequence, a true love does occur when Rosader and Rosalynd exchange looks.

Unlike Shakespeare in *As You Like It*, Lodge makes issues of rank and politics continue to affect the promptings of his characters. When Rosalynd first recognises she is in love, her first thoughts, when she is alone and able to reflect, are for the state implications of a possible match:

> thou art poor and without patrimony, and yet the daughter of a prince; he a younger brother, and void of such possessions as either might maintain thy dignities or revenge thy father's injuries.

It is only when she has thought of royalty as power that she can recollect the other tradition of princely magnanimity, of royal ethics: 'Can the degree of a princess, the daughter of Gerismond harbour such servile conceits, as to prize gold more than honour?'

The Torismond version of princeliness has briefly held her mind when she is in his court, but even in the forest similar thoughts occur. There is no magic about this Arden: Alinda and Rosalynd are only momentarily free from the pressures of power. 'Thus will I live quiet, unknown and contented', Alinda can say, but two sentences later we hear that Montanus sat meanwhile 'in a muse, thinking of the cruelty of his Phoebe'. There is a personal politics in the forest parallel to the demands of power at court. Alinda does not take to being contradicted by Rosalynd, as we have seen. Rosalynd, meeting Rosader again, can only think that love may renew not the miseries of the court, but the pain of losing it: 'for that thou art in exile and banished from the court whose distress, as it is appeased with patience, so it would be renewed with amorous passions'.

Pastoral in *Rosalynd* is only a momentary holiday for the courtly characters who take advantage of a cleaner world of more spontaneous feelings, but continue to think as men and women of rank. Gerismond does not read sermons in stones like Shakespeare's Duke Senior, but waits for the inevitable uprising to restore him. When the news of it is brought to the wedding feast by brother number two, it turns out that this king has everything ready for the event, 'I have horse and armour for us all', and when Alinda cries out to him to be generous to her father, Lodge dryly observes his haste to be gone: 'he not returning a word because his haste was great'. If Saladyn and Rosader are restored to family feeling, unlike the war to the death in *Gamelyn*, Lodge still sees to it that the youngest brother's restoration to primacy, the justification of the legacy, still matters. When Ganymede's identity as Rosalynd is revealed, Saladyn is put into 'a dump' and Alinda, still in disguise, comments with surprising directness: 'Perchance thou art sorrowful to think on thy brother's high fortunes and thine own base desires to choose so mean a shepherdess.' When she also reveals her identity, Gerismond, without any rebuke to Saladyn, offers him congratulations: 'Then', quoth Gerismond turning to Saladyn, 'jolly forester be frolic, for thy fortunes are great, and thy desires excellent. Thou hast got a princess.' It is the 'then' that is so striking; only if fortune is great does desire also become excellent, apparently. The fairy tale of the forester and the princess is adjusted in the light of this reality. But anyway the restoration of Gerismond turns Rosader into the future King of France, where Saladyn has in the end to be content to be Duke of Nameurs. The concern with money and rank is neither moral oversight nor obtuseness in the text. Lodge presents the readers with the problems created by very different systems of value and refuses to sort them out. He writes a text strewn with small dilemmas to be pondered.

So, in a way not totally unlike *Gamelyn* after all, younger brothers thrive in *Rosalynd* and end up not king's favourites, but kings themselves. The tensions are there in the original legacy which speaks of family unity yet favours one brother over the others and appeals to values both of contentment and honour, stillness and striving. There is no wonder that the *Gamelyn* story commanded Lodge's particular interest. He was himself a younger son, the second, to a rich man later declared bankrupt.[5] When he was around four years old, in 1562, his father, also Thomas, became Lord Mayor of London, like the boy's natural grandfather before him, and was knighted shortly afterwards. He had a finger in Elizabethan pies of varied wholesomeness – the reform of currency, the foundation of the Muscovy Company, but also the start of the slave trade, in his year of office, with Hawkins's first venture. But the son obviously fell into family disfavour. After Trinity College, Oxford (BA, 1577), he went on to Lincoln's Inn in 1578, but seems early to have abandoned his law studies for the excitements and precariousness of literary life in London. He was a friend of Barnabe Rich and Greene, with whom he collaborated. When his mother died in 1578, he was left legacies, to mature when he reached

---

5.   W. D. Rae, *Thomas Lodge* (New York, 1967); E. A. Tenney, *Thomas Lodge* (Ithaca, 1935).

twenty-five, dependent on his proceeding to his examinations. These bequests were not mentioned in his father's will in 1583, nor was anything left to him from that source. The range of his work, from a formal elegy for his mother to an attack on money-lenders in *An Alarum Against Usurers* (1584), speaks of a typical career on the edge of the book market. He sailed on a freebooting expedition with Captain Clarke to the Canaries and Azores in 1588, the voyage mentioned in the preface to *Rosalynd*, and later accompanied Cavendish to the straits of Magellan and Brazil in 1591. On his return in 1593, he again attempted to earn a living by his pen but appears to have given up after 1596. In 1597 he was in Avignon, where he studied medicine, became a Catholic and returned to London to practise, mainly among his fellow recusants.

The details of his life command attention because they typify the difficulties of the graduate who refused to follow the younger son's route of the Church and the quest for a lucrative stipend or the law and the search for employment as a man of business to some magnate. The problem of this educated second son, given the changes of historical circumstance, turns out to be not so far from Gamelyn's. Training prepared young men for the service of the state, but they often found that the state did not require their services or they acquired an interest in literature as a means of getting attention and then had to scramble through the dingy paths of Elizabethan Grub Street. How many students in our present-day university intake who declare an interest in journalism or broadcasting are actually going to make their living by these? Disappointment fostered a critical stance that found fuel in their reading of ancient rhetoric, in the writings of Cicero and Seneca. The topics of Latin satire also seemed dangerously applicable in the closing decades of the century to a London of extravagant display and shady enterprise. Lodge's father had fallen foul of the court over a matter of requisitioned catering and suffered a reverse at law over the disputed possession of twelve capons. The mixture of peril and pure farce must have required all the straightness of face implicit in the formalities of the Elizabethan prose that his son was writing to survive in such a dangerous world.

Lodge was one of the first authors of formal verse satire and his prose works are as extensively critical as Nashe's. The constant undercurrents of threat and violence and divergence of values that trouble the smooth surface of *Rosalynd* give it its argumentative heart. Along with *Scylla's Metamorphosis*, an Ovidian erotic narrative, he published in 1589 a series of satires, one of which was a pastoral invitation to retirement from the world into a landscape where the hermit sees what the women find in the prose tale of the following year:

> Whether with solace tripping on the trees
> He sees the citizens of Forest sport,
> Or midst the withered oak beholds the bees
> Intend their labour with a kind comfort.[6]

But he also includes a semi-dramatised speech by a satyr in a similar wooded glade transformed by night, which expresses a particular dislike for Cynthia, the moon-goddess, so often used by contemporary poets as a compliment to Elizabeth herself, and a prayer instead to the unfamiliar goddess, Discontent:

> The mind through thee divines on endless things,
> And forms a Heaven through others' fond mislikes.[7]

Ambition and *Schadenfreude* are fuelled by her, but are themselves the source of creativity. Even writers themselves are subject to her inspiration:

> You studious arts, how fatal haps had you
> If discontents did not some succours yield?
> Oh fleeting Fame, who could thy grace pursue,
> Did not my God send emulations out
> To whet the wits and pens of Pallas' rout?

The clumsiness, as with many of the poems in *Rosalynd*, springs from the tongue stumbling over too much to say, not from vacuous inattention. Like many other mock encomiums of the time, the writing charges what is offered as the untrustworthy words of, ostensibly, a semi-demon with a witty delight, as though the writer has been liberated by saying the unsayable. At the end of the poem the apparently disapproving speaker says he tried to imitate the gaiety of the speaker who, by acknowledging Discontent as a god, has become a 'lightfoot faun'. Ambition troubles and inspires most of the figures in *Rosalynd* in one way or another and even in Montanus discontent is transformed into love-complaint. The equivalent to Shakespeare's Jacques is Adam's general description of life's conditions when he and Rosader are starving in the forest:

> All our pleasures end in pain and our highest delights are crossed with deepest discontents. The joys of man, as they are few, so are they momentary, scarce ripe before they are rotten, and withering in the blossom, either parched with the heat of envy or fortune.

---

6. *Tudor Verse Satire*, ed. W. K. Gransden (London, 1970), p.91.
7. Ibid, p. 88.

What complicates the moral generalisation here is the sense that pleasure itself generates its own destruction, even as it is achieved, either out of ourselves or others' 'deepest discontents' or 'envy'. That is the other voice to the story's fusion of success in love with political reward.

What makes the difference to the outline of the *Gamelyn* story and its implications is the blessed introduction of female characters, of which there is not one in the medieval poem. Lodge's address, like that in many romances of the time, is specifically to his gentlemen readers and he flatters them in the story by the amount of space he gives to the women's feelings for the men. Rosalynd and Alinda are free and sportive, but what they principally freely do is fall in love with Rosader and Saladyn. The interplay between surrender and liberty gives the analysis of love in the tale an unusual sprightliness. Rosalynd is caught out by her feelings not because she has not loved before, but because she has and thinks she understands how to gauge her emotions:

> she accounted love a toy and fancy a momentary passion, that as it was taken in with a gaze might be shaken off with a wink, and therefore feared not to dally in the flame.

The angry earnestness of the male emotions in the original narrative are not more real than the feelings of the women in Lodge, but Rosalynd and Alinda watch themselves having their emotions and control at least the moment and the way in which they will disclose them. By becoming Ganymede playing at being Rosalynd, the woman can both express her genuine feelings and prevent her maybe-intended partner from quite hearing them, as within the verse-game of the eclogue. The disguise is used not so much to tease Rosader about the nature of love as such, as in *As You Like It*, as to acknowledge fully her own emotions, much faster than Shakespeare's Rosalind, and yet preserve distance and control. When Alinda teases her with accepting Rosader so straightforwardly, Rosalynd retreats immediately into her role as page-boy:

> 'Tush,' quoth Ganymede, 'all is not malt that is cast on the kiln; there goes more words to a bargain than one; love feels no footing in the air and fancy holds it slippery harbour to nestle in the tongue; the match is not yet so surely made but he may miss of his market; but if Fortune be his friend, I will not be his foe.'

The brisk no-nonsense maxims imply a male world of commercial transaction where the honourable belief that your word is your bond holds no ground. What is so deleterious in the relation of the brothers, that Saladyn's word never 'nestles in the tongue', becomes here the means available to Rosalynd in her male role to provide the illusion of freedom, though she intends to be loyal. The canny weighing of advantage, 'If fortune be his friend', speaks a prudence that she has already dispensed with, finding in the disguise itself a practical prudence to trust.

In this game of gender, Alinda's role is equally as important as Rosalynd's. It is she who, when the peers are afraid of Torismond, can brave her father's anger in defending her friend from the charge of treason. Her attachment to her friend challenges the instances of male devotion and the world will 'speak of Rosalynd and Alinda as they did of Pylades and Orestes'. It is her idea to run off to the forest and she becomes the employer, a sheep-farmer in her own right. She has a bigger part in the story than Celia in Shakespeare's play, partly because Saladyn is a bigger role than Oliver. The speed with which she knows and makes known her feelings expresses, within the varieties of love offered in the tale, a gracious statement of strong and unclouded passion. We should not expect authorial comment from Lodge, but in Alinda's combination of self-sacrifice, resourcefulness and good-humour he is presenting, by external evidence rather than interior analysis, a woman of formidable character. Even in the ending she stands a little apart: 'Alinda being very passionate for the death of her father, yet brooking it with the more patience in that she was contented with the welfare of her Saladyn'. Fortune does not obliterate feeling.

Rosalynd is really two stories in one, then, a dark male narrative and a bright female one, but, unlike Shakespeare's confinement of the first tale basically to Act One, Lodge keeps elements from it in the foreground until half-way through the work, with Saladyn's banishment. The result is to turn the whole book into a kind of debate about the sources and inspirations of conduct and the relative weight of emulation as against love, say. In this, it reinterprets the implications of the sub-title *Euphues' Golden Legacy*, in as much as Sir John's legacy is revalued in the tale itself. In the second of his prose compositions, *Euphues and his England* (1580), Lyly offers two prefaces, the first 'To the Ladies and Gentlewomen of England' and the other 'To the Gentlemen Readers'. Granted the differences of tone – slightly insolent rallying with the women, defensive aggression with the men – he implies a difference of major interest between the sexes. He expects the women to read the book as an analysis of the varieties of love – 'divers questions and quirks of love' – and the men to be interested in the rhetorical methods displayed: 'All my discourses shall be regarded, some for the smell, some for the smart, all for a kind of a loving smack.'[8] But Lyly is much more concerned with the second of these, and his analysis of passion is critical and dismissive, the expression of what George

---

8. *Euphues*, ed. Edward Arber (London, 1868), p. 224.

Hunter calls 'the learned tradition of misogyny'.[9] Even in the commendatory letter Lyly prefaced to Thomas Watson's *Hekatompathia* (1582), he can say sourly:

> Were not men more superstitious in their praises, than women are constant in their passions: Love would either shortly be worn out of use, or men out of love, or women out of lightness.[10]

If *Rosalynd* is to be attributed to Euphues, then he has changed his mind and, in a death-bed repentance, has altered his conception of women in love even from the second part. Lodge's tale has less interest in moral discourse for its own sake and trusts more to the opportunities afforded by the tale itself. The varieties of love are enormously expanded to cover not simply the three different love stories as such, but the family feeling of the brothers, Gerismond's love for his daughter, and the love between the women – 'Aliena as merry as might be that she was thus in the company of her Rosalynd', for example.

By developing the element of story, Lodge turns the Euphuistic oration into a dramatic moment of self-realisation with a decisive recoil from one argument to another. The pattern is set by Saladyn's first meditation as he thinks about the property left to his younger brothers and the father's command that they love one another:

> 'No Saladyn, entreat them with favours, and entertain them with love, so shalt thou have thy conscience clear and thy renown excellent. Tush, what words are these, base fool, far unfit (if thou be wise) for thy humour?'

The arguments cut through each other under the impulse of contradictory valuations. The desire for a good conscience becomes almost immediately a kind of timidity from the other point of view, the action of a man who could be addressed as 'base fool', a man of low desires. When Rosader finds his sleeping brother in the forest about to be savaged by the lion, he first wants to think that the gods have acted on his behalf without any intervention by himself, 'But he had not stepped back two or three paces but a new motion struck him to the very heart.' Alinda, in love with Saladyn, finds irony in the recognition that at court the pleasures of courtship meant nothing to her, but that now she lives in a cottage love strikes:

---

9. G. K. Hunter, *John Lyly: The Humanist as Courtier* (London, 1962), p. 31.
10. Thomas Watson, *Poems*, ed. Edward Arber (London, 1910), p. 30.

'I have heard them say, that Love looks not at low cottages, that Venus jets in robes not in rags, that Cupid flies so high that he scorns to touch poverty with his heel. Tush, Alinda, these are but old wives' tales, and neither authentical precepts nor infallible principles'.

Wittily she answers her own fear that there is no rustic Venus as itself a rustic superstition, an old wife's tale. The fears that Lodge gives his characters come not from the scholar's repertoire of commonplaces, but directly out of the narrative – Saladyn's jealousy as eldest son, Rosader's desire for revenge, Alinda's ambiguous social rank.

They are not dramatically realised, though they have dramatic causes; the style is not torn apart by the fierceness of the internal debate. They are verbal icons of dilemma rather than representations of passion. But the stylised form should not disguise from us the intelligence at work in the presentation of people making discoveries in these speeches, finding that they are saying what they never expected to utter. Defending Rosalynd before her father, Alinda suddenly claims that if it can really be proved that her friend is a traitor, 'let her die, and Alinda will execute the massacre', which is indeed what her slightly fierce personality might produce as a thought. Saladyn, cast in prison by Torismond, reflects that though the cause is unjust, the effect is a right punishment for his treatment of Rosader; persecuted himself, he has sudden sympathy for the subject of his own persecution. Adam Spencer, worn out by disappointment that the escape to the forest produced only starvation, lets his mind run over the futilities of life until all that is left seems to be suicide. Montanus, so accustomed to the passivities of his role as lover, begs his rival Ganymede to marry Phoebe to prevent her feeling what he feels himself.

Isocolon, the rhetorical figure which balances one element of the structure against another, is not a Euphuistic tic for Lodge, but the way in which his mind works in the narrative as a whole as well as in the detail of its writing. The aesthetic of balance holds in check the variety of attitude and the diversity of impulse which the work embodies. The harmony of the prose lends easy access to the lyrics that spring from it. Henry Peacham comments on 'compar', as he calls the figure:

When the members of an oration, be almost of a just number of syllables, but yet equality of the parts or numbers must not be measured upon our fingers, but be tried by a secret sense of the ear.[11]

The desire is for euphony, 'to make the numbers accord very well and pleasantly', and, as usual in this rhetoric, Peacham adduces scriptural

---

11. Henry Peacham, *The Garden of Eloquence* (London, 1577), sig. K1r.

instances, especially from the structure of Hebrew poetry: 'Through me do princes bear rule, and all judges of the earth execute judgements.' Puttenham famously recommends the figure as giving good grace to prose, though he limits its use to no more than three or four such clauses in succession.[12] Lodge does not vary the style for his different speakers and Corydon the old shepherd will speak in it and produce his Latin quotations as much as Rosader or Alinda. It is not that he has only one way of writing prose; the easy graciousness of the address to Hunsdon sounds entirely different from the brusque familiarity of the speech to the readers, and both are unlike the text of the tale itself. But the story itself is a narration which makes no attempt to conceal its single written identity. Indeed, when the two women in Arden first catch sight of Montanus and Corydon, the writer invites the reader suddenly to take their place: 'Drawing more nigh we might descry the countenance of the one to be full of sorrow ... We, to hear what these were, stole privily behind the thicket, where we overheard this discourse.' The style enforces on the reader a self-consciousness like that of the characters. The even *impasto*, silkily smooth, increases our detailed observation which, however disputably, is obviously a means to encourage habits of attentiveness.

Yet there remains a distance for the reader to travel between the method and assumptions of what remain essentially two stories, the activity and violence of the *Gamelyn* tale, with its dour expectations of betrayal and greed, and the comparative slowness and stillness of the forest story where the major business is love. Lodge magnifies that difference of scale by his introduction of the two kings into the *Gamelyn* tale – not brothers as in Shakespeare, we should note. He took the names from a tragedy by Tasso set in a mythical Norway. Torismond's usurpation of the kingdom writes politically large Saladyn's attempts to disinherit his brothers. However, affairs can be got right at the private level which then have consequences politically. But even in the forest, Ganymede unintentionally dispossesses Montanus of Phoebe's affections. Ganymede-Rosalynd cannot be tempted by the offer, of course, but the speed with which she finds a way to help the futile Montanus, whose sacrifice of his own feelings in pleading Phoebe's case gives him sudden interest, puts the actions of the political world to shame. In this mingling of private with political judgements, Lodge is influenced by Sidney's *Arcadia*, which appeared in print the same year as *Rosalynd* but was available in its original form, written around 1580, in many manuscripts by the late 80s. Affairs of state and the negotiations of love constantly overlap in Sidney. So, just as Saladyn in prison recognises his own guilt towards Rosader, Phoebe can learn from her own pain

---

12. George Puttenham, *The Arte of English Poesie* (London, 1589), pp. 178–9.

a fellow-feeling for Montanus which is closer to loving him than she has ever been before: 'So deeply I repent me of my frowardness toward the shepherd, that could I cease to love Ganymede, I would resolve to like Montanus.' As in *Arcadia*, the characters are forced by their mischances into disguise, including cross-dressing, but the consequences here are to encourage an unwonted honesty; Saladyn's confession of what he feels he has done wrong is the more moving to Rosader because it is made as to a stranger.

If *Rosalynd* is one huge narrative isocolon, then the other leg of it derives from the tradition of serious pastoral of which *Arcadia* is the great example. In Sidney's original version, however, most of the poems are confined to the close of each of its five books and form a narrative in themselves parallel to the main plot. Other than Sir John's epitaph, the lyrics in Lodge's story express the loving feelings of the main characters on specific occasions; they are the other voice to the developed oratory of the meditations, passions and discourses. They are closer in function to the self-conscious demonstration of poetic skills by the shepherds in Jorge de Montemayor's immensely popular *Diana* (?1559).[13] Knowledge of Spanish was comparatively more widely spread in later sixteenth-century England than it is now; Lodge certainly knew Spanish at a later date and anyway there were early translations into French. Poems from *Diana* were used by Barnabe Googe as early as 1563 and it was admired greatly by Sidney. The name of Montanus may derive from the identical denomination of a particularly anguished shepherd in Selvagia's story which ends Book I of the *Diana* and returns later in the continuation by Gil Polo. But in de Montemayor numerous story lines constantly interrupt each other and delay the resolutions of the unhappy complications to which all the shepherds are subject. Lodge lets the pastoral temper alter the sense of time in *Rosalynd* to a degree. The days are shaped by the progress of the sun rather than by specific actions: 'Every day leading forth her flocks, with such delight that she held her exile happy'. It is that reconstruction of time in terms of Alinda's experience of repetitions, 'every day', rather than the unique shaping of causes and effects which is the primary fact of pastoral. Its business becomes conversation and lyric. But in that case, *As You Like It* is more determinedly pastoral than *Rosalynd*, where the love affairs are brisk and the actions keep returning us to the political story. To Lodge, the landscape of the Ardennes is partly an unlocated place of lemon groves and lions, but also a recognisable forest that acts as a barrier on the road to Lyons for Saladyn and provides food

---

13. *A Critical Edition of Yong's Translation of … Diana*, ed. Judith M. Kennedy (Oxford, 1968), p. xxxix.

at its outer limits but offers few resources to Rosader and Adam at the dense heart of it. If the rival king has his court in it, it also shelters genuine outlaws who try to kidnap Alinda and Rosalynd. The double identity is in many ways more like that of the native pastoral of Spenser's *Shepheardes Calendar*, as are the two long eclogues between Corydon and Montanus and Rosader and Rosalynd. It is the comparative urgency, speed and happiness of Lodge's version of pastoral which make the work so distinctive; he avoids the delays of interlaced narrative.

But the book's happiness cannot disguise the problems it accommodates. Its moral conclusion comes as a surprise by returning to the issue of the father's legacy, as well as that of Euphues, and by the extent to which it does not quite fit the story we have read. 'Such as neglect their father's precepts incur much prejudice' seems an odd comment on Saladyn's mistreatment at the hands of a tyrant and his eventual destiny as Duke of Nameurs. It reminds us that Sir John had told his sons 'to be loyal to your prince' without specifying which of the two he meant. Both kings claim acquaintance with the old knight. When Torismond discovers Rosader's identity after the wrestling bout, he honours him as his father's son, though Gerismond in the forest claims that Sir John had been his old friend. Unless the father's precepts had been disobeyed, the story as we have it could not have been resolved so happily. That is partly the general providence under which all the stories, and life itself, operates. But *Rosalynd*, compared with most pastorals, dispenses with magic and seeks to make its coincidences explicable. To a peculiar degree, that makes the directing agency into fortune which turns out to be providential. When the problem of Montanus comes before Gerismond for judgement, he turns to Ganymede and says: 'Let us hear your argument'. But the argument turns out after all to be an action, Rosalynd resuming her woman's dress. The precepts of Sir John's will could never have brought about such a delight, beyond all expectation; everything happens through the creativity of discontent and the crooked byways of the action. When little seems to be happening, during the daily recurrences of the forest, the problems of the action are being secretly resolved.

Rosalynd offers a harsher world than *As You Like It*: its interest is not wholly absorbed by providing a source for that play and it has something left over after it has been raided by Shakespeare scholars. It is typical of it that the success of Gerismond and his party at the end should depend on 'the fury of their weapons'. In its metamorphosis of pain into pleasure, the cost is counted in ways that are in fact more like Shakespeare's last plays. It may lack a Jacques, but momentary sorrows, bitterness and hard realities invade even the fastnesses of its forest.

ROSALYND.

Euphues' Golden Legacy:

found after his death in his cell at Silexedra.

Bequeathed to Philautus' sons,

nursed up with their father in England.[1]

Fetched from the Canaries by T[homas] L[odge], Gent.

LONDON, Imprinted by Thomas Orwin

for T. G. and John Busbie.
1590.

---

1. Lodge signals that his text is to be considered as a successor to John Lyly's
    popular prose romances of *Euphues*.

TO THE RIGHT HO-

nourable and his most esteemed
Lord the Lord of Hunsdon, Lord
Chamberlain of her Majesty's
household, and Governor of her
Town of Berwick:
T. L. G. wisheth increase
of all honourable vir-
tues.[1]

Such Romans (right Honourable) as delighted in martial exploits attempted their actions in the honour of Augustus,[2] because he was a patron of soldiers and Virgil dignified him with his poems as a Maecenas[3] of scholars, both jointly advancing his royalty as a prince warlike and learned. Such as sacrifice to Pallas[4] present her with bays[5] as she is wise and with armour as she is valiant, observing herein that excellent *to prepon*[6] which dedicateth honours according to the perfection of the person. When I entered (right Honourable) with a deep insight into the consideration of these premises, seeing your L[ordship] to be a patron of all martial men and a Maecenas of such as apply themselves to study, wearing with Pallas both the lance and the bay, and aiming with Augustus at the favour of all by the honourable virtues of your mind; being myself first a student, and after falling from books to arms, even vowed in all my thoughts dutifully to affect your L[ordship]. Having with Capt. Clarke made a voyage to the islands of Terceras[7] and the Canaries, to beguile the time with labour I writ this book; rough, as hatched in the storms of the ocean, and feathered in the surges of many perilous seas. But as it is the work of a soldier and a scholar, I presumed to shroud it under your Honour's patronage, as one that is the fautor[8] and favourer of all virtuous actions, and whose honourable loves, grown from the general applause of the whole commonwealth for your higher deserts, may keep it from the malice of every bitter

---

1. The dedicatee is the same Lord Chamberlain who became patron of Shakespeare's acting company. 'T. L. G.' stands for Thomas Lodge, Gentleman.
2. Augustus] The first Roman emperor; presided over the richest period of ancient Roman history.
3. Maecenas] Roman statesman; adviser to Augustus and patron of Horace.
4. Pallas] Pallas Athena; the martial and wise Greek goddess.
5. bays] The bay laurel was worn on the head as an emblem of victory and honour in classical times.
6. *to prepon*] Greek: decorum.
7. Terceras] Terceira, an island in the North Atlantic in the Azores.
8. fautor] A protector, patron.

tongue. Other reasons more particular (right Honourable) challenge in me a special affection to your L[ordship], as being a scholar with your two noble sons Master Edmund Carew and M. Robert Carew (two scions worthy of so honourable a tree, and a tree glorious in such honourable fruit), as also being scholar in the university under that learned and virtuous knight Sir Edward Hoby[1] when he was Bachelor in Arts, a man as well lettered as well born, and after the etymology of his name soaring as high as the wings of knowledge can mount him, happy every way, and the more fortunate as blessed in the honour of so virtuous a lady. Thus (right Honourable) the duty that I owe to the sons chargeth me that all my affection be placed on the father; for where the branches are so precious, the tree of force must be most excellent. Commanded and emboldened thus with the consideration of these forepassed reasons to present my book to your Lordship, I humbly entreat your Honour will vouch of my labours, and favour a soldier's and a scholar's pen with your gracious acceptance; who answers in affection what he wants in eloquence, so devoted to your Honour as his only desire is to end his life under the favour of so martial and learned a patron.

Resting thus in hope of your Lordship's courtesy in deigning the patronage of my work, I cease, wishing you as many honourable fortunes as your Lordship can desire or I imagine.

Your Honour's soldier
humbly affectionate:
Thomas Lodge.

To the Gentlemen Readers.

Gentlemen, look not here to find any sprigs of Pallas' bay tree, nor to hear the humour of any amorous laureate, nor the pleasing vein of any eloquent orator; *Nolo altum sapere*,[2] they be matters above my capacity. The cobbler's check[3] shall never light on my head; *Ne sutor ultra crepidam*,[4] I will go no further than the latchet,[5] and then all is well. Here you may

---

1. Hoby] Pronounced 'Hobby', thus punning on the bird of prey of that name.
2. *Nolo altum sapere*] Latin: I have no wish to understand profundities.
3. cobbler's check] Refers to the proverbial saying, 'Let not the cobbler/shoemaker go beyond his last.'
4. *Ne sutor ultra crepidam*] Latin: Let the cobbler stick to his last.
5. latchet] From the phrase 'To go above and beyond one's latchet'; to meddle with what does not concern one.

perhaps find some leaves of Venus' myrtle,[1] but hewn down by a soldier with his curtal axe,[2] not bought with the allurement of a filed tongue. To be brief, Gentlemen, room for a soldier, and a sailor that gives you the fruits of his labours that he wrought in the ocean when every line was wet with a surge and every humorous passion counterchecked with a storm. If you like it, so; and yet I will be yours in duty, if you be mine in favour. But if Momus[3] or any squint-eyed ass that hath mighty ears to conceive with Midas,[4] and yet little reason to judge, if he come aboard our bark[5] to find fault with the tackling when he knows not the shrouds,[6] I'll down into the hold and fetch out a rusty poleaxe[7] that saw no sun this seven year, and either well baste him or heave the coxcomb[8] overboard to feed cods. But courteous Gentlemen that favour most, backbite none, and pardon what is overslipt, let such come and welcome, I'll into the stewards' room and fetch them a can of our best beverage. Well Gentlemen, you have Euphues' Legacy. I fetched it as far as the islands of Terceras, and therefore read it, censure with favour, and farewell.

Yours T. L.

The Schedule[9] *annexed to Euphues' Testament,*
the tenor of his legacy, the token of his love.

The vehemency of my sickness, Philautus, hath made me doubtful of life, yet must I die in counselling thee like Socrates, because I love thee. Thou hast sons by Camilla, as I hear, who being young in years have green thoughts, and nobly born have great minds: bend them in their youth like the willow, lest thou bewail them in their age for their wilfulness. I have bequeathed them a golden legacy because I greatly love thee. Let them read it as Archelaus[10] did Cassander,[11] to profit by it, and in reading let

---

1. Venus' myrtle] The myrtle plant was held sacred to Venus and is used as an emblem of love.
2. curtal axe] Obsolete term for cutlass.
3. Momus] Greek myth; the god of blame and mockery.
4. Midas] Greek legend; King of Phrygia. When judging a musical contest between Apollo and Pan, Midas decided against Apollo, who thereupon gave him asses' ears to indicate his stupidity.
5. bark] Or barque; a sailing ship of three or more masts.
6. shrouds] Pattern of ropes used to stay a mast.
7. poleaxe] A kind of axe formerly used as a weapon of war.
8. coxcomb] A conceited fool; a fop.
9. *Schedule*] Codicil to a will. This section was first printed in the edition of 1592.
10. Archelaus] King of Macedon, *c.* 413–399 BC.
11. Cassander] Macedonian ruler.

them meditate, for I have approved it the best method. They shall find love anatomised by Euphues with as lively colours as in Apelles'[1] table; roses to whip him when he is wanton, reasons to withstand him when he is wily. Here may they read that virtue is the king of labours, opinion the mistress of fools, that unity is the pride of Nature, and contention the overthrow of families. Here is hellebore bitter in taste, but beneficial in trial. I have nothing to send thee and Camilla but this counsel: that instead of worldly goods, you leave your sons virtue and glory, for better were they to be partakers of your honours than lords of your manors. I feel death that summoneth me to my grave, and my soul desirous of his god. Farewell Philautus, and let the tenor of my counsel be applied to thy childrens' comfort.

Euphues dying to live.

If any man find this scroll, send it to Philautus in England.

ROSALYND

There dwelt adjoining to the city of Bordeaux a knight of most honourable parentage, whom Fortune had graced with many favours, and Nature honoured with sundry exquisite qualities, so beautified with the excellence of both, as it was a question whether Fortune or Nature were more prodigal in deciphering the riches of their bounties. Wise he was, as holding in his head a supreme conceit of policy, reaching with Nestor[2] into the depth of all civil government, and to make his wisdom more gracious, he had that *salem ingenii*[3] and pleasant eloquence that was so highly commended in Ulysses.[4] His valour was no less than his wit, nor the stroke of his lance no less forcible than the sweetness of his tongue was persuasive, for he was for his courage chosen the principal of all the knights of Malta.[5] This hardy knight thus enriched with virtue and honour, surnamed Sir John of Bordeaux, having passed the prime of his youth in sundry battles against the Turks, at last (as the date of time hath his course)

---

1. Apelles] Greek painter of mythological subjects.
2. Nestor] Greek myth; an elder statesman and the oldest and wisest of the Greeks in the Trojan war.
3. *salem ingenii*] Latin: shrewd wit.
4. Ulysses] Greek myth; one of the foremost of the Greek heroes at the siege of Troy, noted for his rhetorical skill.
5. knights of Malta] A military religious order.

grew aged. His hairs were silver-hued and the map of age was figured on his forehead; honour sat in the furrows of his face, and many years were portrayed in his wrinkled lineaments that all men might perceive his glass was run and that Nature of necessity challenged her due. Sir John (that with the phoenix knew the term of his life was now expired, and could with the swan discover his end by her songs) having three sons by his wife Lynida, the very pride of all his forepassed years, thought now (seeing death by constraint would compel him to leave them) to bestow upon them such a legacy as might bewray his love and increase their ensuing amity. Calling therefore these young gentlemen before him in the presence of all his fellow knights of Malta, he resolved to leave them a memorial of his fatherly care in setting down a method of their brotherly duties. Having therefore death in his looks to move them to pity, and tears in his eyes to paint out the depth of his passions, taking his eldest son by the hand he began thus.

Sir John of Bordeaux' Legacy
he gave to his sons

'O my sons, you see that Fate hath set a period of my years, and destinies have determined the final end of my days; the palm tree waxeth awayward, for he stoopeth in his height, and my plumes are full of sick feathers touched with age. I must to my grave that dischargeth all cares, and leave you to the world that increaseth many sorrows. My silver hairs containeth great experience, and in the number of my years are penned down the subtleties of Fortune. Therefore as I leave you some fading pelf[1] to countercheck poverty, so I will bequeath you infallible precepts that shall lead you unto virtue. First therefore unto thee Saladyn, the eldest and therefore the chiefest pillar of my house, wherein should be engraven as well the excellence of thy father's qualities as the essential form of his proportion, to thee I give fourteen ploughlands with all my manor houses and richest plate. Next unto Fernandyn I bequeath twelve ploughlands. But unto Rosader, the youngest, I give my horse, my armour and my lance, with sixteen ploughlands; for if the inward thoughts be discovered by outward shadows, Rosader will exceed you all in bounty and honour. Thus, my sons, have I parted in your portions the substance of my wealth, wherein if you be as prodigal to spend as I have been careful to get, your friends will grieve to see you more wasteful than I was bountiful, and your foes smile that my fall did begin in your excess. Let mine honour be the glass of your actions, and the fame of my virtues the lodestar[2] to direct the course of

---

1. pelf] Property or possessions.
2. lodestar] Literally, guiding star; something that serves as a guide or model.

your pilgrimage. Aim your deeds by my honourable endeavours, and show yourselves scions[1] worthy of so flourishing a tree, lest, as the birds halcyons[2] which exceed in whiteness, I hatch young ones that surpass in blackness. Climb not, my sons: aspiring pride is a vapour that ascendeth high, but soon turneth to a smoke. They which stare at the stars, stumble upon stones, and such as gaze at the sun (unless they be eagle-eyed) fall blind. Soar not with the hobby,[3] lest you fall with the lark, nor attempt not with Phaethon,[4] lest you drown with Icarus.[5] Fortune when she wills you to fly, tempers your plumes with wax, and therefore either sit still and make no wing, or else beware the sun and hold Daedalus' axiom authentical (*medium tenere tutissimum*).[6] Low shrubs have deep roots, and poor cottages great patience. Fortune looks ever upward, and envy aspireth to nestle with dignity. Take heed, my sons, the mean is sweetest melody, where strings high stretched either soon crack or quickly grow out of tune. Let your country's care be your heart's content, and think that you are not born for yourselves but to level your thoughts to be loyal to your prince, careful for the common weal, and faithful to your friends; so shall France say, "These men are as excellent in virtues as they be exquisite in features." O my sons, a friend is a precious jewel, within whose bosom you may unload your sorrows and unfold your secrets, and he either will relieve with counsel or persuade with reason; but take heed in the choice, the outward show makes not the inward man, nor are the dimples in the face the calendars of truth. When the liquorice leaf looketh most dry, then it is most wet; when the shores of Lepanthus are most quiet, then they forepoint a storm. The Baaran leaf[7] the more fair it looks, the more infectious it is, and in the sweetest words is oft hid the most treachery. Therefore my sons, choose a friend as the Hyperboreans[8] do the metals, sever them from the ore with fire, and let them not bide the stamp before they be current. So try and then trust, let time be touchstone of friendship,

---

1. scions] A shoot or twig of a plant; also a descendent, heir or young member of a family.
2. halcyons] Greek myth; a fabulous bird associated with the winter solstice.
3. hobby] Small falcon.
4. Phaethon] Greek myth; son of Helios, the sun god, who borrowed his father's chariot and nearly set the earth on fire by getting too close to it.
5. Icarus] Greek myth; son of Daedalus, with whom he escaped from Crete flying with waxen wings. Heedless of his father's warning, he flew too close to the sun, his wings melted and he fell into the sea and drowned.
6. *medium tenere tutissimum*] Latin: It is safest to keep the mean.
7. Baaran leaf] Alluring but poisonous vegetable matter.
8. Hyperboreans] A fabulous people believed by the Greeks to live a blessed existence in the distant, inaccessible north.

and then friends faithful lay them up for jewels. Be valiant, my sons, for cowardice is the enemy to honour; but not too rash, for that is an extreme. Fortitude is the mean, and that is limited within bonds and prescribed with circumstance. But above all,' and with that he fetched a deep sigh, 'beware of love, for it is far more perilous than pleasant, and yet I tell you it allureth as ill as the Sirens.[1] O my sons, fancy is a fickle thing, and beauty's paintings are tricked up with time's colours, which, being set to dry in the sun, perish with the same. Venus is a wanton, and though her laws pretend liberty, yet there is nothing but loss and glistering misery. Cupid's wings are plumed with the feathers of vanity, and his arrows, where they pierce, enforce nothing but deadly desires. A woman's eye, as it is precious to behold, so it is prejudicial to gaze upon, for as it affordeth delight, so it snareth unto death. Trust not their fawning favours, for their loves are like the breath of a man upon steel, which no sooner lighteth on but it leapeth off, and their passions are as momentary as the colours of a polyp[2] which changeth at the sight of every object. My breath waxeth short and mine eyes dim; the hour is come and I must away, therefore let this suffice: women are wantons, and yet men cannot want one, and therefore if you love, choose her that hath her eyes of adamant that will turn only to one point, her heart of a diamond that will receive but one form, her tongue of a sethin leaf that never wags but with a southeast wind; and yet, my sons, if she have all these qualities, to be chaste, obedient, and silent, yet for that she is a woman shalt thou find in her sufficient vanities to countervail her virtues. O now, my sons, even now take these my last words as my latest legacy, for my thread is spun and my foot is in the grave. Keep my precepts as memorials of your father's counsels and let them be lodged in the secret of your hearts, for wisdom is better than wealth, and a golden sentence worth a world of treasure. In my fall see and mark, my sons, the folly of man, that being dust climbeth with Biares[3] to reach at the heavens, and ready every minute to die yet hopeth for an age of pleasures. Oh, man's life is like lightning that is but a flash, and the longest date of his years but as a bavin's blaze.[4] Seeing then man is so mortal, be careful that thy life be virtuous, that thy death may be full of admirable honours; so shalt thou challenge fame to be thy fautor,[5] and put oblivion to exile with thine honourable actions. But, my sons, lest you should forget your

---

1. Sirens] Greek myth; female characters who had the power of drawing men to destruction by their song.
2. polyp] Piece of coral.
3. Biares] Error for Briareus, one of the giants in Greek myth who aided Zeus in overthrowing the Titans.
4. bavin] Brushwood, firewood.   5. fautor] Patron.

father's axioms, take this scroll, wherein read what your father dying wills you to execute living.' At this he shrunk down in his bed and gave up the ghost.

John of Bordeaux being thus dead was greatly lamented of his sons and bewailed of his friends, especially of his fellow knights of Malta, who attended on his funerals, which were performed with great solemnity. His obsequies done, Saladyn caused, next his epitaph, the contents of the scroll to be portrayed out, which were to this effect:

The contents of the Schedule which Sir John of Bordeaux gave to his Sons

My sons, behold what portion I do give;
I leave you goods, but they are quickly lost;
I leave advice, to school you how to live;
I leave you wit, but won with little cost:
But keep it well, for counsel still is one,
When father, friends, and worldly goods are gone.

In choice of thrift let honour be thy gain,
Win it by virtue and by manly might;
In doing good esteem thy toil no pain,
Protect the fatherless and widow's right:
Fight for thy faith, thy country and thy king,
For why? this thrift will prove a blessed thing.

In choice of wife, prefer the modest-chaste;
Lilies are fair in show, but foul in smell;
The sweetest looks by age are soon defaced;
Then choose thy wife by wit and living well.
Who brings thee wealth and many faults withal,
Presents thee honey, mixed with bitter gall.

In choice of friends, beware of light belief;
A painted tongue may shroud a subtle heart;
The Siren's tears do threaten mickle [1] grief;
Foresee, my son, for fear of sudden smart:
Choose in thy wants, and he that friends thee then,
When richer grown, befriend him thou again.

---

1. mickle] A great quantity or amount.

Learn of the ant in summer to provide;
Drive with the bee the drone from out thy hive;
Build like the swallow in the summer tide;
Spare not too much (my son) but sparing thrive:
Be poor in folly, rich in all but sin:
So by thy death thy glory shall begin.

Saladyn having thus set up the schedule, and hanged about his father's hearse many passionate poems, that France might suppose him to be passing sorrowful, he clad himself and his brothers all in black, and in such sable suits discoursed his grief. But as the hyena when she mourns is then most guileful, so Saladyn under this show of grief shadowed a heart full of contented thoughts. The tiger, though he hide his claws, will at last discover his rapine; the lion's looks are not the maps of his meaning, nor a man's physiognomy is not the display of his secrets. Fire cannot be hid in the straw, nor the nature of man so concealed but at last it will have his course. Nurture and art may do much, but that *Natura naturans*[1] which by propagation is engrafted in the heart, will be at last perforce predominant according to the old verse:

Naturam expellas furca licet, tamen usque recurret.[2]

So fared it with Saladyn, for after a month's mourning was passed, he fell to consideration of his father's testament, how he had bequeathed more to his younger brothers than himself, that Rosader was his father's darling but now under his tuition, that as yet they were not come to years and he being their guardian, might (if not defraud them of their due) yet make such havoc of their legacies and lands as they should be a great deal the lighter, whereupon he began thus to meditate with himself:

Saladyn's meditation with himself

'Saladyn, how art thou disquieted in thy thoughts and perplexed with a world of restless passions, having thy mind troubled with the tenor of thy father's testament and thy heart fired with the hope of present preferment. By the one thou art counselled to content thee with thy fortunes, by the other persuaded to aspire to higher wealth. Riches, Saladyn, is a great royalty, and there is no sweeter physic than store. Avicen,[3] like a fool,

---

1. *Natura naturans*] Latin: spirit of nature.
2. *Naturam ... recurret*] Latin: Though you drive Nature out with a pitch-fork, she will come right back (Horace, *Epistles*, 1.10.24).
3. Avicen] Ancient philosopher and commentator on Aristotle.

forgot in his aphorisms to say that gold was the most precious restorative and that treasure was the most excellent medicine of the mind. O Saladyn, what, were thy father's precepts breathed into the wind? Hast thou so soon forgot his principles? Did he not warn thee from coveting without honour and climbing without virtue? Did he not forbid thee to aim at any action that should not be honourable? And what will be more prejudicial to thy credit than the careless ruin of thy brothers' welfare? Why, shouldst not thou be the pillar of thy brothers' prosperity, and wilt thou become the subversion of their fortunes? Is there any sweeter thing than concord or a more precious jewel than amity? Are you not sons of one father, scions of one tree, birds of one nest, and wilt thou become so unnatural as to rob them whom thou shouldst relieve? No Saladyn, entreat them with favours and entertain them with love, so shalt thou have thy conscience clear and thy renown excellent. Tush, what words are these, base fool, far unfit (if thou be wise) for thy humour. What though thy father at his death talked of many frivolous matters, as one that doted for age and raved in his sickness, shall his words be axioms and his talk be so authentical that thou wilt (to observe them) prejudice thy self? No, no, Saladyn, sick men's wills that are parole[1] and have neither hand nor seal, are like the laws of a city written in dust, which are broken with the blast of every wind. What man, thy father is dead, and he can neither help thy fortunes, nor measure thy actions; therefore bury his words with his carcase and be wise for thyself. What, 'tis not so old as true,

Non sapit, qui sibi non sapit.[2]

Thy brother is young, keep him now in awe, make him not checkmate with thyself, for

Nimia familiaritas contemptum parit.[3]

Let him know little, so shall he not be able to execute much; suppress his wits with a base estate, and though he be a gentleman by nature, yet form him anew and make him a peasant by nurture. So shalt thou keep him as a slave, and reign thyself sole lord over all thy father's possessions. As for Fernandyn, thy middle brother, he is a scholar and hath no mind but on Aristotle – let him read on Galen[4] while thou riflest with gold, and pore

---

1.   parole] The pleadings in an action when presented by word of mouth.
2.   *Non ... sapit*] Latin: He is not wise who knows not himself.
3.   *Nimia ... parit*] Latin: Too much familiarity breeds contempt.
4.   Galen] Greek physician, anatomist and physiologist whose authority continued into the Renaissance.

on his book till thou dost purchase lands. Wit is great wealth; if he have learning it is enough, and so let all rest.'

In this humour was Saladyn making his brother Rosader his foot-boy for the space of two or three years, keeping him in such servile subjection as if he had been the son of any country vassal. The young gentleman bore all with patience, till on a day walking in the garden by himself he began to consider how he was the son of John of Bordeaux, a knight renowned for many victories, and a gentleman famed for his virtues; how, contrary to the testament of his father, he was not only kept from his land and entreated as a servant, but smothered in such secret slavery as he might not attain to any honourable actions. 'Ah,' quoth he to himself (nature working these effectual passions), 'why should I that am a gentleman born, pass my time in such unnatural drudgery? Were it not better either in Paris to become a scholar, or in the court a courtier, or in the field a soldier, than to live a foot-boy to my own brother? Nature hath lent me wit to conceive, but my brother denied me art to contemplate; I have strength to perform any honourable exploit, but no liberty to accomplish my virtuous endeavours; those good parts that God hath bestowed upon me, the envy of my brother doth smother in obscurity; the harder is my fortune, and the more his frowardness.' With that casting up his hand he felt hair on his face, and perceiving his beard to bud, for choler he began to blush, and swore to himself he would be no more subject to such slavery. As thus he was ruminating of his melancholy passions in came Saladyn with his men, and seeing his brother in a brown study,[1] and to forget his wonted reverence, thought to shake him out of his dumps thus: 'Sirrah,' quoth he, 'what is your heart on your halfpenny, or are you saying a dirge for your father's soul? What, is my dinner ready?' At this question Rosader, turning his head askance and bending his brows as if anger there had ploughed the furrows of her wrath, with his eyes full of fire, he made this reply: 'Dost thou ask me, Saladyn, for thy cates?[2] Ask some of thy churls who are fit for such an office. I am thine equal by nature, though not by birth, and though thou hast more cards in the bunch, I have as many trumps in my hands as thyself. Let me question with thee why thou hast felled my woods, spoiled my manor houses, and made havoc of such utensils as my father bequeathed unto me? I tell thee, Saladyn, either answer me as a brother or I will trouble thee as an enemy.'

At this reply of Rosader's, Saladyn smiled as laughing at his presumption, and frowned as checking his folly; he therefore took him up thus shortly: 'What sirrah, well I see early pricks the tree that will prove a thorn.

---

1. brown study] A mood of deep absorption or thoughtfulness.
2. cates] Choice dainty food; delicacies.

Hath my familiar conversing with you made you coy, or my good looks drawn you to be thus contemptuous? I can quickly remedy such a fault, and I will bend the tree while it is a wand. In faith, sir boy, I have a snaffle for such a headstrong colt. You, sirs, lay hold on him and bind him, and then I will give him a cooling card for his choler.' This made Rosader half mad, that stepping to a great rake that stood in the garden, he laid such load upon his brother's men that he hurt some of them and made the rest of them run away. Saladyn, seeing Rosader so resolute and with his resolution so valiant, thought his heels his best safety and took him to a loft adjoining to the garden, whither Rosader pursued him hotly. Saladyn, afraid of his brother's fury, cried out to him thus: 'Rosader, be not so rash, I am thy brother and thine elder, and if I have done thee wrong I'll make thee amends: revenge not anger in blood, for so shalt thou stain the virtue of old Sir John of Bordeaux. Say wherein thou are discontent and thou shalt be satisfied. Brothers' frowns ought not to be periods of wrath. What, man, look not so sourly; I know we shall be friends, and better friends than we have been, for, *Amantium irae amoris redintegratio est.*[1]

These words appeased the choler of Rosader (for he was of a mild and courteous nature) so that he laid down his weapons, and upon the faith of a gentleman assured his brother he would offer him no prejudice. Whereupon Saladyn came down, and after a little parley they embraced each other and became friends, and Saladyn promising Rosader the restitution of all his lands, 'and what favour else' (quoth he) 'any ways my ability or the nature of a brother may perform'. Upon these sugared reconciliations they went into the house arm in arm together, to the great content of all the old servants of Sir John of Bordeaux. Thus continued the pad[2] hidden in the straw, till it chanced that Torismond king of France had appointed for his pleasure a day of wrestling and of tournament to busy his commons' heads, lest being idle their thoughts should run upon more serious matters and call to remembrance their old banished king. A champion there was to stand against all comers, a Norman, a man of tall stature and of great strength, so valiant that in many such conflicts he always bare away the victory, not only overthrowing them which he encountered, but often with the weight of his body killing them outright. Saladyn hearing of this, thinking now not to let the ball fall to the ground, but to take opportunity by the forehead, first by secret means convented with the Norman, and procured him with rich rewards to swear that if Rosader came within his claws he should never more return to quarrel with Saladyn for his possessions. The Norman desirous of pelf, as (*Quis*

---

1. *Amantium … est*] Latin: Lovers' quarrels are the renewal of love (Terence, *Andria*, 555). 2. pad] Poisonous toad.

nisi mentis inops oblatum respuit aurum?)[1] taking great gifts for little gods, took the crowns of Saladyn to perform the strategem. Having thus the champion tied to his villainous determination by oath, he prosecuted the intent of his purpose thus. He went to young Rosader (who in all his thoughts reached at honour and gazed no lower than virtue commanded him) and began to tell him of this tournament and wrestling, how the king should be there, and all the chief peers of France, with all the beautiful damsels of the country: 'Now brother,' quoth he, 'for the honour of Sir John of Bordeaux our renowned father, to famous that house that never hath been found without men approved in chivalry, show thy resolution to be peremptory. For myself, thou knowest though I am eldest by birth, yet never having attempted any deeds of arms, I am youngest to perform any martial exploits, knowing better how to survey my lands than to charge my lance. My brother Fernandyn he is at Paris poring on a few papers, having more insight into sophistry and principles of philosophy, than any warlike endeavours; but thou, Rosader, the youngest in years but the eldest in valour, art a man of strength and darest do what honour allows thee. Take thou my father's lance, his sword, and his horse, and hie thee to the tournament, and either there valiantly crack a spear, or try with the Norman for the palm of activity.' The words of Saladyn were but spurs to a free horse, for he had scarce uttered them ere Rosader took him in his arms, taking his proffer so kindly that he promised in what he might to requite his courtesy. The next morrow was the day of the tournament, and Rosader was so desirous to show his heroical thoughts that he past the night with little sleep, but as soon as Phoebus[2] had vailed the curtain of the night and made Aurora[3] blush with giving her the *bezo les labres*[4] in her silver couch, he got him up, and taking his leave of his brother, mounted himself towards the place appointed, thinking every mile ten leagues till he came there. But leaving him so desirous of the journey – to Torismond the king of France, who having by force banished Gerismond their lawful king that lived as an outlaw in the forest of Arden, sought now by all means to keep the French busied with all sports that might breed their content. Amongst the rest he had appointed this solemn tournament, whereunto he in most solemn manner resorted, accompanied with the twelve peers of France, who, rather for fear than love, graced him with the show of their dutiful favours. To feed their eyes, and to make the beholders pleased with the sight of most rare and glistering objects, he had appointed his

---

1. *Quis ... aurum*] Latin: Who but the weak of mind refuses offered gold?
2. Phoebus] Greek myth; Phoebus Apollo, the god of light.
3. Aurora] Roman goddess of the dawn.
4. *bezo les labres*] French: kiss the lips.

own daughter Alinda to be there, and the fair Rosalynd, daughter unto Gerismond, with all the beautiful damsels that were famous for their features in all France. Thus in that place did love and war triumph in a sympathy, for such as were martial might use their lance to be renowned for the excellence of their chivalry, and such as were amorous might glut themselves with gazing on the beauties of most heavenly creatures. As every man's eye had his several survey, and fancy was partial in their looks, yet all in general applauded the admirable riches that Nature bestowed on the face of Rosalynd, for upon her cheeks there seemed a battle between the Graces, who should bestow most favours to make her excellent. The blush that gloried Luna [1] when she kissed the shepherd on the hills of Latmos was not tainted with such a pleasant dye as the vermilion flourished on the silver hue of Rosalynd's countenance; her eyes were like those lamps that make the wealthy covert of the heavens more gorgeous, sparkling favour and disdain, courteous and yet coy, as if in them Venus had placed all her amorets [2] and Diana [3] all her chastity. The trammels [4] of her hair, folded in a caul [5] of gold, so far surpassed the burnished glister of the metal as the sun doth the meanest star in brightness. This Rosalynd sat I say with Alinda as a beholder of these sports, and made the cavaliers crack their lances with more courage. The tresses that folds in the brows of Apollo were not half so rich to the sight, for in her hair it seemed Love had laid herself in ambush to entrap the proudest eye that durst gaze upon their excellence. What should I need to decipher her particular beauties, when by the censure of all she was the paragon of all earthly perfection? Many deeds of knighthood that day were performed, and many prizes were given according to their several deserts. At last when the tournament ceased, the wrestling began, and the Norman presented himself as a challenger against all comers. But he looked like Hercules [6] when he advanced himself against Achelous, so that the fury of his countenance amazed all that durst attempt to encounter with him in any deed of activity, till at last a lusty franklin [7] of the country came with two tall men

---

1. Luna] Roman goddess of the moon.
2. amorets] Looks that inspire love; love glances.
3. Diana] Ancient Italian female divinity, the moon goddess; patroness of virginity and hunting.
4. trammels] Plaits, braids or tresses of a woman's hair.
5. caul] Netted cap.
6. Hercules] Roman adaptation of the Greek hero Heracles, who competed with the river god, Achelous, for the love of Deiamira.
7. franklin] A freeholder; used in the fourteenth and fifteenth centuries to designate a class of landowners of free but not noble birth, ranking next below the gentry.

that were his sons, of good lineaments and comely personage. The eldest of these doing his obeisance to the king entered the list and presented himself to the Norman, who straight coped with him and as a man that would triumph in the glory of his strength, roused himself with such fury that not only he gave him the fall, but killed him with the weight of his corpulent personage: which the younger brother seeing, leapt presently into the place, and thirsty after the revenge, assailed the Norman with such valour that at the first encounter he brought him to his knees; which repulsed so the Norman that, recovering himself, fear of disgrace doubling his strength, he stepped so sternly to the young franklin that, taking him up in his arms, he threw him against the ground so violently that he broke his neck, and so ended his days with his brother. At this unlooked-for massacre the people murmured and were all in a deep passion of pity, but the franklin, father unto these, never changed his countenance, but as a man of a courageous resolution, took up the bodies of his sons without any show of outward discontent. All the while stood Rosader and saw this tragedy, who noting the undoubted virtue of the franklin's mind, alighted off from his horse, and presently sat down on the grass and commanded his boy to pull off his boots, making him ready to try the strength of the champion. Being furnished as he would, he clapped the franklin on the shoulder and said thus: 'Bold yeoman, whose sons have ended the term of their years with honour, for that I see thou scornest fortune with patience and thwartest the injury of fate with content in brooking the death of thy sons, stand awhile and either see me make a third in their tragedy, or else revenge their fall with an honourable triumph.' The franklin, seeing so goodly a gentleman to give him such courteous comfort, gave him hearty thanks with promise to pray for his happy success. With that Rosader vailed bonnet[1] to the king and lightly leapt within the lists, where noting more the company than the combatant, he cast his eye upon the troop of ladies that glistered there like the stars of heaven. But at last Love, willing to make him as amorous as he was valiant, presented him with the sight of Rosalynd, whose admirable beauty so inveigled the eye of Rosader that forgetting himself he stood and fed his looks on the favour of Rosalynd's face; which she perceiving blushed, which was such a doubling of her beauteous excellence that the bashful red of Aurora at the sight of unacquainted Phaethon was not half so glorious. The Norman seeing this young gentleman fettered in the looks of the ladies, drove him out of his *memento*[2] with a shake by the shoulder. Rosader looking back with an angry frown, as if he had been wakened from some pleasant dream,

---

1. vailed bonnet] Took off his hat as a mark of respect.
2. *memento*] Latin: reverie.

discovered to all by the fury of his countenance that he was a man of some high thoughts; but when they all noted his youth and the sweetness of his visage, with a general applause of favours, they grieved that so goodly a young man should venture in so base an action: but seeing it were to his dishonour to hinder him from his enterprise, they wished him to be graced with the palm of victory. After Rosader was thus called out of his *memento* by the Norman, he roughly clapped to him with so fierce an encounter that they both fell to the ground, and with the violence of the fall were forced to breathe; in which space the Norman called to mind by all tokens that this was he whom Saladyn had appointed him to kill, which conjecture made him stretch every limb and try every sinew, that working his death he might recover the gold which so bountifully was promised him. On the contrary part, Rosader while he breathed was not idle but still cast his eye upon Rosalynd, who to encourage him with a favour lent him such an amorous look as might have made the most coward desperate; which glance of Rosalynd so fired the passionate desires of Rosader that turning to the Norman he ran upon him and braved him with a strong encounter. The Norman received him as valiantly that there was a sore combat, hard to judge on whose side fortune would be prodigal. At last Rosader, calling to mind the beauty of his new mistress, the fame of his father's honours, and the disgrace that should fall to his house by his misfortune, roused himself and threw the Norman against the ground, falling upon his chest with so willing a weight that the Norman yielded nature her due, and Rosader the victory. The death of this champion, as it highly contented the franklin as a man satisfied with revenge, so it drew the king and all the peers into a great admiration, that so young years and so beautiful a personage should contain such martial excellence. But when they knew him to be the youngest son of Sir John of Bordeaux, the king rose from his seat and embraced him, and the peers entreated him with all favourable courtesy, commending both his valour and his virtues, wishing him to go forward in such haughty deeds that he might attain to the glory of his father's honourable fortunes. As the king and lords graced him with embracing, so the ladies favoured him with their looks, especially Rosalynd, whom the beauty and valour of Rosader had already touched; but she accounted love a toy and fancy a momentary passion, that as it was taken in with a gaze might be shaken off with a wink, and therefore feared not to dally in the flame; and to make Rosader know she affected him, took from her neck a jewel and sent it by a page to the young gentleman. The prize that Venus gave to Paris[1] was not half so pleasing to the Trojan as

---

1. Paris] Greek myth; son of Priam King of Troy and his wife Hecuba. The 'prize' that Venus gave to Paris was Helen of Troy.

this gem was to Rosader, for if fortune had sworn to make him sole monarch of the world, he would rather have refused such dignity than have lost the jewel sent him by Rosalynd. To return her with the like he was unfurnished, and yet that he might more than in his looks discover his affection, he stepped into a tent, and taking pen and paper wrote this fancy:

Two suns at once from one fair heaven there shined,
Ten branches from two boughs tipped all with roses,
Pure locks more golden than is gold refined,
Two pearled rows that Nature pride encloses;

Two mounts fair marble-white, down-soft and dainty,
A snow-dyed orb, where love increased by pleasure
Full woeful makes my heart, and body fainty:
Her fair, my woe, exceeds all thought and measure.

In lines confused my luckless harm appeareth,
Whom sorrow clouds, whom pleasant smiling cleareth.

This sonnet he sent to Rosalynd, which when she read she blushed, but with a sweet content in that she perceived love had allotted her so amorous a servant. Leaving her to her new entertained fancies, again to Rosader, who triumphing in the glory of this conquest, accompanied with a troop of young gentlemen that were desirous to be his familiars, went home to his brother Saladyn's, who was walking before the gates to hear what success his brother Rosader should have, assuring himself of his death, and devising how with dissimuled sorrow to celebrate his funerals. As he was in this thought, he cast up his eye and saw where Rosader returned with the garland on his head, as having won the prize, accompanied with a crew of boon companions. Grieved at this, he stepped in and shut the gate. Rosader seeing this, and not looking for such unkind entertainment, blushed at the disgrace, and yet smothering his grief with a smile, he turned to the gentlemen and desired them to hold his brother excused, for he did not this upon any malicious intent or niggardise, but being brought up in the country he absented himself, as not finding his nature fit for such youthful company. Thus he sought to shadow abuses proffered him by his brother, but in vain, for he could by no means be suffered to enter; whereupon he ran his foot against the door and broke it open, drawing his sword and entering boldly into the hall, where he found none (for all were fled) but one Adam Spencer, an Englishman who had been an old and trusty servant to Sir John of Bordeaux. He, for the love he bore to his deceased master, favoured the part of Rosader, and gave him and his such entertainment as he could. Rosader gave him thanks, and looking about, seeing the hall empty, said, 'Gentlemen, you are welcome; frolic and be merry, you shall be sure to have wine enough whatsoever your fare be; I tell you, cavaliers, my brother hath in his house five tun[1] of wine, and as long as it lasteth I beshrew[2] him that spares his liquor.' With that he burst open the buttery[3] door, and with the help of Adam Spencer, covered the tables and set down whatsoever he could find in the house, but what they wanted in meat, Rosader supplied with drink, yet had they royal cheer, and withal such a hearty welcome as would have made the coarsest meats seem delicates. After they had feasted and frolicked it twice or thrice with an upsee freeze,[4] they all took their leaves of Rosader and departed. As soon as they were gone, Rosader, growing impatient of the abuse, drew his sword and swore to be revenged on the discourteous Saladyn, yet by the means of Adam Spencer, who sought to continue friendship and amity betwixt the brethren, and through the flattering submission of Saladyn, they were once again reconciled, and put up all forepassed injuries with a peaceable agreement, living together for a good space in such brotherly love as did not only rejoice the servants, but made all the gentlemen and bordering neighbours glad of such friendly concord. Saladyn, hiding fire in the straw, and concealing a poisoned hate in a peaceable countenance, yet deferring the intent of his wrath till fitter opportunity, he showed himself a great favourer of his brother's virtuous endeavours – where leaving them in this happy league, let us return to Rosalynd.

Rosalynd returning home from the triumph, after she waxed solitary, love presented her with the idea of Rosader's perfection, and taking her at discovert,[5] struck her so deep as she felt herself grow passing passionate. She began to call to mind the comeliness of his person, the honour of his parents, and the virtues that, excelling both, made him so gracious in the eyes of everyone. Sucking in thus the honey of love, by imprinting in her thoughts his rare qualities, she began to surfeit with the contemplation of his virtuous conditions, but when she called to remembrance her present estate, and the hardness of her fortunes, desire began to shrink and fancy to vail bonnet, that between a chaos of confused thoughts, she began to debate with herself in this manner:

---

1. tun] large cask (equivalent to 4 hogsheads, capacity 216 imperial (= 252 US) gallons).
2. beshrew] To curse.
3. buttery] A place for storing liquor; from an early period the name also extended to 'the room where provisions are laid up'.
4. upsee freeze] A mode of drinking or carousing.
5. discovert] An uncovered or exposed state.

'Unfortunate Rosalynd, whose misfortunes are more than thy years, and whose passions are greater than thy patience! The blossoms of thy youth are mixed with the frosts of envy, and the hope of thy ensuing fruits perish in the bud. Thy father is by Torismond banished from the crown, and thou, the unhappy daughter of a king, detained captive, living as disquieted in thy thoughts as thy father discontented in his exile. Ah Rosalynd, what cares wait upon a crown! What griefs are incident to dignity! What sorrows haunt royal palaces! The greatest seas have the sorest storms, the highest birth subject to the most bale, and of all trees the cedars soonest shake with the wind; small currents are ever calm, low valleys not scorched in any lightnings, nor base men tied to any baleful prejudice. Fortune flies, and if she touch poverty it is with her heel, rather disdaining their want with a frown than envying their wealth with disparagement. O Rosalynd, hadst thou been born low, thou hadst not fallen so high; and yet being great of blood, thine honour is more if thou brookest misfortune with patience. Suppose I contrary fortune with content, yet fates unwilling to have me any way happy have forced love to set my thoughts on fire with fancy. Love, Rosalynd! Becometh it women in distress to think of love? Tush, desire hath no respect of persons, Cupid is blind and shooteth at random, as soon hitting a rag as a robe, and piercing as soon the bosom of a captive as the breast of a libertine. Thou speakest it, poor Rosalynd, by experience, for being every way distressed, surcharged with cares, and overgrown with sorrows, yet amidst the heap of all these mishaps, love hath lodged in thy heart the perfection of young Rosader, a man every way absolute as well for his inward life as for his outward lineaments, able to content the eye with beauty, and the ear with the report of his virtue. But consider, Rosalynd, his fortunes, and thy present estate: thou art poor and without patrimony, and yet the daughter of a prince; he a younger brother, and void of such possessions as either might maintain thy dignities or revenge thy father's injuries. And hast thou not learned this of other ladies, that lovers cannot live by looks, that women's ears are sooner content with a dram of *give me* than a pound of *hear me*, that gold is sweeter than eloquence, that love is a fire and wealth is the fuel, that Venus' coffers should be ever full. Then Rosalynd, seeing Rosader is poor, think him less beautiful because he is in want, and account his virtues but qualities of course, for that he is not endued with wealth. Doth not Horace tell thee what method is to be used in love,

---

1. *Passion*] A poem, literary composition, or passage marked by deep or strong emotion.

Quaerenda pecunia primum, post nummos virtus.[1]

Tush, Rosalynd, be not over rash, leap not before thou look; either love such a one as may with his lands purchase thy liberty, or else love not at all. Choose not a fair face with an empty purse, but say as most women use to say,

Si nihil attuleris, ibis Homere foras.[2]

Why Rosalynd, can such base thoughts harbour in such high beauties? Can the degree of a princess, the daughter of Gerismond harbour such servile conceits as to prize gold more than honour, or to measure a gentleman by his wealth, not by his virtues? No, Rosalynd, blush at thy base resolution and say, if thou lovest, either Rosader or none. And why? Because Rosader is both beautiful and virtuous.' Smiling to herself to think of her new-entertained passions, taking up her lute that lay by her, she warbled out this ditty:

Rosalynd's Madrigal.

> Love in my bosom like a bee
>   doth suck his sweet:
> Now with his wings he plays with me,
>   now with his feet.
>   Within mine eyes he makes his nest,
>   His bed amidst my tender breast,
>   My kisses are his daily feast;
>   And yet he robs me of my rest.
>   Ah wanton, will ye?
>
> And if I sleep, then percheth he
>   with pretty flight,
> And makes his pillow of my knee
>   the livelong night.
>   Strike I my lute, he tunes the string,
>   He music plays if so I sing,
>   He lends me every lovely thing;
>   Yet cruel he my heart doth sting.
>   Whist, wanton, still ye!

---

1. *Quaerenda ... virtus*] Latin: Seek money first, virtue after cash.
2. *Si ... foras*] Latin: If you bring nothing, out you go Homer.

Else I with roses every day
　　will whip you hence,
And bind you when you long to play,
　　for your offence.
I'll shut mine eyes to keep you in,
I'll make you fast it for your sin,
I'll count your power not worth a pin;
Alas, what hereby shall I win,
　　If he gainsay me?

What if I beat the wanton boy
　　with many a rod?
He will repay me with annoy,
　　because a god.
Then sit thou safely on my knee,
And let thy bower my bosom be;
Lurk in mine eyes, I like of thee.
O Cupid, so thou pity me,
　　Spare not but play thee.

Scarce had Rosalynd ended her madrigal before Torismond came in with his daughter Alinda, and many of the peers of France, who were enamoured of her beauty; which Torismond perceiving, fearing lest her perfection might be the beginning of his prejudice, and the hope of his fruit end in the beginning of her blossoms, he thought to banish her from the court: 'For', quoth he to himself, 'her face is so full of favour that it pleads pity in the eye of every man, her beauty is so heavenly and divine that she will prove to me as Helen did to Priam; some one of the peers will aim at her love, end the marriage, and then in his wife's right attempt the kingdom. To prevent therefore *had I wist* in all these actions, she tarries not about the court, but shall (as an exile) either wander to her father, or else seek other fortunes.' In this humour, with a stern countenance full of wrath, he breathed out this censure unto her before the peers, that charged her that that night she were not seen about the court: 'for', quoth he, 'I have heard of thy aspiring speeches and intended treasons.' This doom was strange unto Rosalynd, and presently, covered with the shield of her innocence, she boldly broke out in reverent terms to have cleared herself; but Torismond would admit of no reason, nor durst his lords plead for Rosalynd, although her beauty had made some of them passionate, seeing the figure of wrath portrayed in his brow. Standing thus all mute, and Rosalynd amazed, Alinda who loved her more than herself, with grief in her heart and tears in her eyes, falling down on her knees began to entreat her father thus:

Alinda's Oration to her father
in defence of fair Rosalynd.

'If, mighty Torismond, I offend in pleading for my friend, let the law of amity crave pardon for my boldness, for where there is depth of affection, there friendship alloweth a privilege. Rosalynd and I have been fostered up from our infancies, and nursed under the harbour of our conversing together with such private familiarities that custom had wrought an union of our nature, and the sympathy of our affections such a secret love that we have two bodies and one soul. Then marvel not, great Torismond, if seeing my friend distressed I find myself perplexed with a thousand sorrows, for her virtuous and honourable thoughts (which are the glories that maketh women excellent) they be such as may challenge love and raze out suspicion. Her obedience to your majesty I refer to the censure of your own eye, that since her father's exile hath smothered all griefs with patience, and in the absence of nature, hath honoured you with all duty as her own father by nouriture, not in word uttering any discontent, nor in thought (as far as conjecture may reach) hammering on revenge, only in all her actions seeking to please you and to win my favour. Her wisdom, silence, chastity, and other such rich qualities, I need not decipher: only it rests for me to conclude in one word, that she is innocent. If then, Fortune, who triumphs in variety of miseries, hath presented some envious person (as minister of her intended stratagem) to taint Rosalynd with any surmise of treason, let him be brought to her face and confirm his accusation by witnesses, which proved, let her die, and Alinda will execute the massacre. If none can avouch any confirmed relation of her intent, use justice, my lord, it is the glory of a king, and let her live in your wonted favour; for if you banish her, myself as co-partner of her hard fortunes will participate in exile some part of her extremities.'

Torismond, at this speech of Alinda, covered his face with such a frown as Tyranny seemed to sit triumphant in his forehead, and checked her up with such taunts as made the lords (that only were hearers) to tremble. 'Proud girl,' quoth he, 'hath my looks made thee so light of tongue, or my favours encouraged thee to be so forward, that thou darest presume to preach after thy father? Hath not my years more experience than thy youth, and the winter of mine age deeper insight into civil policy than the prime of thy flourishing days? The old lion avoids the toils where the young one leaps into the net, the care of age is provident and foresees much, suspicion is a virtue where a man holds his enemy in his bosom. Thou, fond girl, measurest all by present affection, and as thy heart loves thy thoughts censure; but if thou knewest that in liking Rosalynd thou hatchest up a bird to peck out thine own eyes, thou wouldst entreat as much for her absence as now thou delightest in her presence. But why do I allege policy to thee? Sit you down, housewife, and fall to your needle: if idleness make you so wanton, or liberty so malapert,[1] I can quickly tie you to a sharper task. And you, maid, this night be packing either into Arden to your father, or whither best it shall content your humour, but in the court you shall not abide.' This rigorous reply of Torismond nothing amazed Alinda, for still she prosecuted her plea in the defence of Rosalynd, wishing her father (if his censure might not be reversed) that he would appoint her partner of her exile, which if he refused to do, either she would by some secret means steal out and follow her, or else end her days with some desperate kind of death. When Torismond heard his daughter so resolute, his heart was so hardened against her that he set down a definitive and peremptory sentence that they should both be banished, which presently was done, the tyrant rather choosing to hazard the loss of his only child than anyways to put in question the state of his kingdom, so suspicious and fearful is the conscience of an usurper. Well, although his lords persuaded him to retain his own daughter, yet his resolution might not be reversed, but both of them must away from the court without either more company or delay. In he went with great melancholy, and left these two ladies alone. Rosalynd waxed very sad, and sat down and wept. Alinda she smiled, and sitting by her friend began thus to comfort her:

Alinda's Comfort to perplexed Rosalynd.

'Why, how now, Rosalynd, dismayed with a frown of contrary fortune? Have I not oft heard thee say that high minds were discovered in fortune's contempt, and heroical scene in the depth of extremities? Thou wert wont to tell others that complained of distress that the sweetest salve for misery was patience, and the only medicine for want, that precious implaister[2] of content. Being such a good physician to others, wilt thou not minister receipts to thyself? But perchance thou wilt say:

Consulenti nunquam caput doluit.[3]

Why then, if the patients that are sick of this disease can find in themselves neither reason to persuade, nor art to cure, yet, Rosalynd, admit of the counsel of a friend, and apply the salves that may appease thy passions. If thou grievest that being the daughter of a prince, and envy thwarteth

---

1. malapert] Of persons, their qualities, actions etc.; presumptuous, impudent, 'saucy'.
2. implaister] Plaster or salve.
3. *Consulenti ... doluit*] Latin: The counsellor's head never aches.

thee with such hard exigents, think that royalty is a fair mark, that crowns have crosses when mirth is in cottages, that the fairer the rose is the sooner it is bitten with caterpillars, the more orient the pearl is the more apt to take a blemish, and the greatest birth, as it hath most honour, so it hath much envy. If then Fortune aimeth at the fairest, be patient, Rosalynd, for first by thine exile thou goest to thy father; nature is higher prized than wealth, and the love of one's parents ought to be more precious than all dignities. Why then doth my Rosalynd grieve at the frown of Torismond, who by offering her a prejudice, proffers her a greater pleasure? And more, mad lass, to be melancholy when thou hast with thee Alinda, a friend who will be a faithful co-partner of all thy misfortunes, who hath left her father to follow thee, and chooseth rather to brook all extremities than to forsake thy presence. What, Rosalynd,

Solamen miseris socios habuisse doloris.[1]

Cheerly, woman: as we have been bedfellows in royalty, we will be fellow-mates in poverty. I will ever be thy Alinda, and thou shalt ever rest to me Rosalynd; so shall the world canonize our friendship, and speak of Rosalynd and Alinda as they did of Pylades[2] and Orestes.[3] And if ever Fortune smile and we return to our former honour, then folding ourselves in the sweet of our friendship, we shall merrily say (calling to mind our forepassed miseries):

Olim haec meminisse iuvabit.[4]

At this Rosalynd began to comfort her, and after she had wept a few kind tears in the bosom of her Alinda, she gave her hearty thanks, and then they sat them down to consult how they should travel. Alinda grieved at nothing but that they might have no man in their company, saying it would be their greatest prejudice in that two women went wandering without either guide or attendant. 'Tush,' quoth Rosalynd, 'art thou a woman, and hast not a sudden shift to prevent a misfortune? I, thou seest, am of a tall stature, and would very well become the person and apparel of a page; thou shalt be my mistress, and I will play the man so properly that, trust me, in what company soever I come I will not be discovered; I will buy me a suit and have my rapier very handsomely at my side, and if any knave

---

1. *Solamen ... doloris*] Latin: It is solace to the wretched to have companions in woe.
2. Pylades] Greek myth; the constant friend of Orestes.
3. Orestes] Greek myth; son of Agamemnon and Clytemnestra.
4. *Olim ... iuvabit*] Latin: One day it will delight us to remember these things (Virgil, *Aeneid*, 1.203).

offer wrong, your page will show him the point of his weapon.' At this Alinda smiled, and upon this they agreed, and presently gathered up all their jewels, which they trussed up in a casket, and Rosalynd in all haste provided her of robes, and Alinda, from her royal weeds, put herself in more homely attire. Thus fitted to the purpose, away go these two friends, having now changed their names, Alinda being called Aliena and Rosalynd Ganymede. They travelled along the vineyards and by many by-ways at last got to the forest side, where they travelled by the space of two or three days without seeing any creature, being often in danger of wild beasts, and pained with many passionate sorrows. Now the black ox began to tread on their feet,[1] and Alinda thought of her wonted royalty, but when she cast her eyes on her Rosalynd, she thought every danger a step to honour. Passing thus on along, about midday they came to a fountain compassed with a grove of cypress trees, so cunningly and curiously planted, as if some goddess had entreated Nature in that place to make her an arbour. By this fountain sat Aliena and her Ganymede, and forth they pulled such victuals as they had and fed as merrily as if they had been in Paris with all the king's delicates, Aliena only grieving that they could not so much as meet with a shepherd to discourse them the way to some place where they might make their abode. At last Ganymede casting up his eye espied where on a tree was engraven certain verses, which as soon as he espied he cried out: 'Be of good cheer, mistress, I spy the figures of men, for here in these trees be engraven certain verses of shepherds, or some other swains that inhabit hereabout.' With that Aliena started up joyful to hear these news and looked, where they found carved in the bark of a pine tree this passion:

Montanus' Passion.

Hadst thou been born whereas perpetual cold
Makes Tanais[2] hard, and mountains silver old;
Had I complain'd unto a marble stone,
Or to the floods bewrayed my bitter moan,
 I then could bear the burden of my grief.
But even the pride of countries at thy birth,
Whil'st heavens did smile, did new array the earth
   with flowers chief.
Yet thou, the flower of beauty blessed born,
Hast pretty looks, but all attir'd in scorn.

---

1.   the black ox began to tread on their feet] 'The black ox has trod on his foot'; misfortune has come to him.
2.   Tanais] The river Don in Russia.

> Had I the power to weep sweet Myrrha's[1] tears,
> Or by my plaints to pierce repining ears;
> Hadst thou the heart to smile at my complaint,
> To scorn the woes that doth my heart attaint,
>> I then could bear the burden of my grief.
> But not my tears, but truth with thee prevails,
> And seeming sour my sorrows thee assails:
>> yet small relief.
> For if thou wilt thou art of marble hard,
> And if thou please my suit shall soon be heard.

'No doubt,' quoth Aliena, 'this poesy is the passion of some perplexed shepherd, that being enamoured of some fair and beautiful shepherdess, suffered some sharp repulse, and therefore complained of the cruelty of his mistress.' 'You may see,' quoth Ganymede, 'what mad cattle you women be, whose hearts sometimes are made of adamant that will touch with no impression, and sometime of wax that is fit for every form. They delight to be courted, and then they glory to seem coy, and when they are most desired then they freeze with disdain, and this fault is so common to the sex that you see it painted out in the shepherd's passions, who found his mistress as froward[2] as he was enamoured.' 'And I pray you,' quoth Aliena, 'if your robes were off, what mettle are you made of that you are so satirical against women? Is it not a foul bird defiles the own nest? Beware, Ganymede, that Rosader hear you not, if he do perchance you will make him leap so far from love that he will anger every vein in your heart.' 'Thus,' quoth Ganymede, 'I keep decorum: I speak now as I am Aliena's page, not as I am Gerismond's daughter; for put me but into a petticoat and I will stand in defiance to the uttermost that women are courteous, constant, virtuous, and what not.' 'Stay there,' quoth Aliena, 'and no more words, for yonder be characters graven upon the bark of the tall beech tree.' 'Let us see,' quoth Ganymede, and with that they read a fancy written to this effect:

> First shall the heavens want starry light,
> The seas be robbed of their waves,
> The days want sun, and sun want bright,
> The night want shade, the dead men graves,
>> The April, flowers and leaf and tree,
>> Before I false my faith to thee.

---

1. Myrrha] Greek myth; daughter of Cinyras, King of Cyprus, to whom she bore a son, Adonis; was metamorphosed into weeping, oozing myrrh tree (denoting tears of penitence).
2. froward] Disposed to go counter to what is demanded or reasonable.

First shall the tops of highest hills
By humble plains be overpried,
And poets scorn the Muses' quills,
And fish forsake the water glide,
    And Iris lose her coloured weed,
    Before I fail thee at thy need.

First direful hate shall turn to peace,
And love relent in deep disdain,
And death his fatal stroke shall cease,
And envy pity every pain,
    And pleasure mourn, and sorrow smile,
    Before I talk of any guile.

First time shall stay his stayless race,
And winter bless his brows with corn,
And snow bemoisten July's face
And winter spring, and summer mourn,
    Before my pen by help of fame,
    Cease to recite thy sacred name.

                    Montanus.

'No doubt,' quoth Ganymede, 'this protestation grew from one full of passions.' 'I am of that mind too,' quoth Aliena, 'but see, I pray, when poor women seek to keep themselves chaste, how men woo them with many feigned promises, alluring with sweet words as the Sirens, and after proving as trothless as Aeneas. Thus promised Demophoon to his Phyllis,[1] but who at last grew more false?' 'The reason was', quoth Ganymede, 'that they were women's sons, and took that fault of their mother, for if man had grown from man, as Adam did from the earth, men had never been troubled with inconstancy.' 'Leave off,' quoth Aliena, 'to taunt thus bitterly, or else I'll pull off your page's apparel and whip you (as Venus doth her wantons) with nettles.' 'So you will,' quoth Ganymede, 'persuade me to flattery and that needs not; but come, seeing we have found here by this fount the tract of shepherds by their madrigals and roundelays,[2] let us forward: for either we shall find some folds, sheepcotes, or else some cottages wherein for a day or two to rest.' 'Content,' quoth Aliena, and with that they rose up and marched forward till towards the even, and then coming into a fair valley, compassed with mountains whereon grew many

---

1.   Demophoon and Phyllis] Story of faithless love in Ovid's *Heroides*.
2.   roundelays] A short, simple song with a refrain.

pleasant shrubs, they might descry where two flocks of sheep did feed. Then, looking about, they might perceive where an old shepherd sat, and with him a young swain, under a covert most pleasantly situated. The ground where they sat was diapered with Flora's[1] riches, as if she meant to wrap Tellus[2] in the glory of her vestments; round about in the form of an amphitheatre were most curiously planted pine trees, interseamed with lemons and citrons, which with the thickness of their boughs so shadowed the place that Phoebus could not pry into the secret of that arbour, so united were the tops with so thick a closure that Venus might there in jollity have dallied unseen with her dearest paramour. Fast by, to make the place more gorgeous, was there a fount so crystalline and clear that it seemed Diana with her Dryads and Hamadryads[3] had that spring as the secret of all their bathings. In this glorious arbour sat these two shepherds, seeing their sheep feed, playing on their pipes many pleasant tunes, and from music and melody falling into much amorous chat. Drawing more nigh we might descry the countenance of the one to be full of sorrow, his face to be the very portraiture of discontent, and his eyes full of woes, that living he seemed to die. We, to hear what these were, stole privily behind the thicket, where we overheard this discourse:

A pleasant Eclogue between Montanus and Corydon.

Corydon.

Say, shepherd's boy, what makes thee greet so sore?
Why leaves thy pipe his pleasure and delight?
Young are thy years, thy cheeks with roses dight:[4]
Then sing for joy, sweet swain, and sigh no more.

This milk-white poppy and this climbing pine
Both promise shade; then sit thee down and sing,
And make these woods with pleasant notes to ring,
Till Phoebus deign all westward to decline.

Montanus.

Ah, Corydon, unmeet is melody
To him whom proud contempt hath overborne:
Slain are my joys by Phoebe's bitter scorn,
Far hence my weal and near my jeopardy.

---

1. Flora] Italian goddess of flowers and spring.
2. Tellus] In Roman religion, the earth goddess, associated with agricultural festivals.
3. Hamadryads] Like Dryads, wood nymphs.
4. dight] Adorned.

Love's burning brand is couched in my breast,
Making a phoenix of my faintful heart:
And though his fury do enforce my smart,
Ay blithe am I to honour his behest.

Prepared to woes since so my Phoebe wills,
My looks dismayed since Phoebe will disdain;
I banish bliss and welcome home my pain:
So stream my tears as showers from Alpine hills.

In error's mask I blindfold judgement's eye,
I fetter reason in the snares of lust,
I seem secure, yet know not how to trust;
I live by that which makes me living die.

Devoid of rest, companion of distress,
Plague to myself, consumed by my thought,
How may my voice or pipe in tune be brought,
Since I am reft of solace and delight?

Corydon.

Ah, lorrel lad,[1] what makes thee hery[2] love?
A sugared harm, a poison full of pleasure,
A painted shrine full filled with rotten treasure,
A heaven in show, a hell to them that prove.

A gain in seeming, shadowed still with want,
A broken staff which folly doth uphold,
A flower that fades with every frosty cold,
An orient rose sprung from a withered plant.

A minute's joy to gain a world of grief,
A subtle net to snare the idle mind,
A seeing scorpion, yet in seeming blind,
A poor rejoice, a plague without relief.

Forthy,[3] Montanus, follow mine arede,[4]
Whom age hath taught the trains that fancy useth,
Leave foolish love, for beauty wit abuseth,
And drowns, by folly, virtue's springing seed.

---

1. lorrel lad] Good-for-nothing.
2. hery] Praise.
3. Forthy] Therefore.
4. arede] Advice.

Montanus.

So blames the child the flame because it burns,
And bird the snare because it doth entrap,
And fools true love because of sorry hap,
And sailors curse the ship that overturns.

But would the child forbear to play with flame,
And birds beware to trust the fowler's gin,
And fools foresee before they fall and sin,
And masters guide their ships in better frame;

The child would praise the fire because it warms,
And bird rejoice to see the fowler fail,
And fools prevent before their plagues prevail,
And sailors bless the bark that saves from harms.

Ah, Corydon, though many be thy years,
And crooked eld[1] hath some experience left,
Yet is thy mind of judgement quite bereft
In view of love, whose power in me appears.

The ploughman little wots to turn the pen,
Or bookman skills to guide the ploughman's cart,
Nor can the cobbler count the terms of art,
Nor base men judge the thoughts of mighty men;

Nor withered age, unmeet for beauty's guide,
Uncapable of love's impression,
Discourse of that whose choice possession
May never to so base a man be tied.

But I, whom nature makes of tender mould,
And youth most pliant yields to fancy's fire,
Do build my haven and heaven on sweet desire,
On sweet desire more dear to me than gold.

Think I of love, oh, how my lines aspire!
How haste the Muses to embrace my brows,
And hem my temples in with laurel boughs,
And fill my brains with chaste and holy fire!

---

1. eld] Old age.

Then leave my lines their homely equipage,
Mounted beyond the circle of the sun:
Amaz'd I read the style [1] when I have done,
And hery love that sent that heavenly rage.

Of Phoebe then, of Phoebe then I sing,
Drawing the purity of all the spheres,
The pride of earth, or what in heaven appears,
Her honoured face and fame to light to bring.

In fluent numbers and in pleasant veins,
I rob both sea and earth of all their state,
To praise her parts: I charm both time and fate,
To bless the nymph that yields me lovesick pains.

My sheep are turned to thoughts, whom froward will
Guides in the restless labyrinth of love;
Fear lends them pasture wheresoe'er they move,
And by their death their life reneweth still.

My sheephook is my pen, mine oaten reed
My paper, where my many woes are written;
Thus silly swain, with love and fancy bitten,
I trace the plains of pain in woeful weed.

Yet are my cares, my broken sleeps, my tears,
My dreams, my doubts, for Phoebe sweet to me:
Who waiteth heaven in sorrow's vale must be,
And glory shines where danger most appears.

Then, Corydon, although I blithe me not,
Blame me not, man, since sorrow is my sweet;
So willeth love, and Phoebe thinks it meet,
And kind Montanus liketh well his lot.

Corydon.
O stayless youth, by error so misguided,
Where will prescribeth laws to perfect wits,
Where reason mourns, and blame in triumph sits,
And folly poisoneth all that time provided!

With wilful blindness bleared, prepared to shame,
Prone to neglect Occasion when she smiles:

---

1. style] Written text.

Alas that love (by fond and forward guiles)
Should make thee tract[1] the path to endless blame!

Ah, my Montanus, cursed is the charm
That hath bewitched so thy youthful eyes:
Leave off in time to like these vanities,
Be forward to thy good, and fly thy harm.

As many bees as Hybla[2] daily shields,
As many fry as fleet on Ocean's face,
As many herds as on the earth do trace,
As many flowers as deck the fragrant fields,

As many stars as glorious heaven contains,
As many storms as wayward winter weeps,
As many plagues as hell enclosed keeps,
So many griefs in love, so many pains.

Suspicions, thoughts, desires, opinions, prayers,
Mislikes, misdeeds, fond joys, and feigned peace,
Illusions, dreams, great pains, and small increase,
Vows, hopes, acceptance, scorns, and deep despairs,

Truce, war, and woe do wait at beauty's gate;
Time lost, lament, reports, and privy grudge,
And last, fierce love is but a partial judge,
Who yields for service shame, for friendship hate.

Montanus.
All adder-like I stop mine ears, fond swain,
So charm no more, for I will never change.
Call home thy flocks in time that straggling range,
For lo, the sun declineth hence amain.

Terentius.

In amore haec omnia insunt vitia: induciae, inimicitiae, bellum, pax rursum: incerta haec si tu postules ratione certa fieri, nihilo plus agas, quam si des operam, ut cum ratione insanias.[3]

---

1. tract] Trace.
2. Hybla] Town in Sicily celebrated for the honey produced on neighbouring hills.
3. *In … insanias*] Latin: In love are all these evils: quarrels, reconcilements, war, then peace again. If you seek by reason to regulate these uncertainties, you will succeed no better than if you set out to reason yourself into madness (from Terence, *Eunuchus*, 1.1.15).

The shepherds having thus ended their eclogue, Aliena stepped with Ganymede from behind the thicket; at whose sudden sight the shepherds arose, and Aliena saluted them thus: 'Shepherds all hail, for such we deem you by your flocks, and lovers good luck, for such you seem by your passions, our eyes being witness of the one, and our ears of the other. Although not by love, yet by Fortune, I am a distressed gentlewoman, as sorrowful as you are passionate, and as full of woes as you of perplexed thoughts. Wandering this way in a forest unknown, only I and my page, wearied with travel, would fain have some place of rest. May you appoint us any place of quiet harbour, be it never so mean, I shall be thankful to you, contented in myself, and grateful to whosoever shall be mine host.' Corydon, hearing the gentlewoman speak so courteously, returned her mildly and reverently this answer:

'Fair mistress, we return you as hearty a welcome as you gave us a courteous salute. A shepherd I am, and this a lover, as watchful to please his wench as to feed his sheep, full of fancies, and therefore (say I) full of follies. Exhort him I may, but persuade him I cannot, for love admits neither counsel nor reason. But leaving him to his passions, if you be distressed, I am sorrowful such a fair creature is crossed with calamity; pray for you I may, but relieve you I cannot. Marry, if you want lodging, if you vouch to shroud yourselves in a shepherd's cottage, my house for this night shall be your harbour.' Aliena thanked Corydon greatly, and presently sat her down and Ganymede by her. Corydon looking earnestly upon her, and with a curious survey viewing all her perfections, applauded in his thought her excellence, and pitying her distress was desirous to hear the cause of her misfortunes, began to question with her thus:

'If I should not, fair damosel, occasion offence, or renew your griefs by rubbing the scar, I would fain crave so much favour as to know the cause of your misfortune, and why and whither you wander with your page in so dangerous a forest.' Aliena, that was as courteous as she was fair, made this reply: 'Shepherd, a friendly demand ought never to be offensive, and questions of courtesy carry privileged pardons in their foreheads. Know therefore, to discover my fortunes were to renew my sorrows, and I should by discoursing my mishaps but rake fire out of the cinders. Therefore let this suffice, gentle shepherd: my distress is as great as my travel is dangerous, and I wander in this forest to light on some cottage where I and my page may dwell, for I mean to buy some farm and a flock of sheep, and so become a shepherdess, meaning to live low and content me with a country life, for I have heard the swains say that they drunk without suspicion and slept without care.' 'Marry, mistress,' quoth Corydon, 'if you mean so you came in a good time, for my landlord intends to sell both the farm I till and the flock I keep, and cheap you may have them for ready money; and for a shepherd's life, O mistress, did you but live a while in their content, you would say the court were rather a place of sorrow than of solace. Here, mistress, shall not Fortune thwart you, but in mean misfortunes, as the loss of a few sheep, which, as it breeds no beggary, so it can be no extreme prejudice: the next year may mend all with a fresh increase. Envy stirs not us, we covet not to climb, our desires mount not above our degrees, nor our thoughts above our fortunes. Care cannot harbour in our cottages, nor do our homely couches know broken slumbers; as we exceed not in diet, so we have enough to satisfy, and, mistress, I have so much Latin, *Satis est quod sufficit.*' [1]

'By my troth, shepherd,' quoth Aliena, 'thou makest me in love with your country life, and therefore send for thy landlord and I will buy thy farm and thy flocks, and thou shalt still under me be overseer of them both. Only for pleasure sake I and my page will serve you, lead the flocks to the field, and fold them: thus will I live quiet, unknown, and contented.' This news so gladdened the heart of Corydon, that he should not be put out of his farm, that (putting off his shepherd's bonnet) he did her all the reverence that he might. But all this while sat Montanus in a muse thinking of the cruelties of his Phoebe, whom he wooed long but was in no hope to win. Ganymede, who still had the remembrance of Rosader in his thoughts, took delight to see the poor shepherd passionate, laughing at love, that in all his actions was so imperious. At last, when she had noted his tears that stole down his cheeks, and his sighs that broke from the centre of his heart, pitying his lament, she demanded of Corydon why the young shepherd looked so sorrowful. 'O sir,' quoth he, 'the boy is in love.' 'Why,' quoth Ganymede, 'can shepherds love?' 'Aye,' quoth Montanus, 'and overlove, else shouldst not thou see me so pensive. Love, I tell thee, is as precious in a shepherd's eye as in the looks of a king, and we country swains entertain fancy with as great delight as the proudest courtier does affection. Opportunity, that is the sweetest friend to Venus, harboureth in our cottages, and loyalty, the chiefest fealty that Cupid requires, is found more among shepherds than higher degrees. Then ask not if such silly swains can love.' 'What is the cause then,' quoth Ganymede, 'that love being so sweet to thee, thou lookest so sorrowful?' 'Because,' quoth Montanus, 'the party beloved is froward, and having courtesy in her looks, holdeth disdain in her tongue's end.' 'What hath she then,' quoth Aliena, 'in her heart?' 'Desire, I hope madam,' quoth he, 'or else, my hope lost, despair in love were death.' As thus they chatted, the sun being ready to set and they not having folded their sheep, Corydon requested she would sit there with her page till Montanus and he lodged their sheep for that night.

---

1. *Satis ... sufficit*] Latin: What suffices is enough.

'You shall go,' quoth Aliena, 'but first I will entreat Montanus to sing some amorous sonnet that he made when he hath been deeply passionate.' 'That I will,' quoth Montanus, and with that he began thus:

Montanus' Sonnet.

Phoebe sat
Sweet she sat,
  Sweet sat Phoebe when I saw her,
White her brow,
Coy her eye:
  Brow and eye how much you please me!
Words I spent,
Sighs I sent,
  Sighs and words could never draw her.
O my love,
Thou art lost,
  Since no sight could ever ease thee.
Phoebe sat
By a fount;
  Sitting by a fount I spied her:
Sweet her touch,
Rare her voice;
  Touch and voice what may disdain you?
As she sung,
I did sigh,
  And by sighs whilst that I tried her,
O mine eyes,
You did lose
  Her first sight whose want did pain you.
Phoebe's flocks
White as wool,
  Yet were Phoebe's locks more whiter.
Phoebe's eyes
Dovelike mild,
  Dovelike eyes both mild and cruel.
Montan swears
In your lamps
  He will die for to delight her.
Phoebe yield,
Or I die;
  Shall true hearts be fancy's fuel?

Montanus had no sooner ended his sonnet but Corydon with a low curtsy rose up and went with his fellow and shut their sheep in the folds, and after returning to Aliena and Ganymede, conducted them home weary to his poor cottage. By the way there was much good chat with Montanus about his loves, he resolving Aliena that Phoebe was the fairest shepherdess in all France, and that in his eye her beauty was equal with the nymphs. 'But,' quoth he, 'as of all stones the diamond is most clearest, and yet most hard for the lapidary[1] to cut, as of all flowers the rose is the fairest, and yet guarded with the sharpest prickles, so of all our country lasses Phoebe is the brightest, but the most coy of all to stoop unto desire. But let her take heed,' quoth he, 'I have heard of Narcissus,[2] who for his high disdain against love perished in the folly of his own love.' With this they were at Corydon's cottage, where Montanus parted from them, and they went in to rest. Alinda and Ganymede, glad of so contented a shelter, made merry with the poor swain, and though they had but country fare and coarse lodging, yet their welcome was so great and their cares so little, that they counted their diet delicate and slept as soundly as if they had been in the court of Torismond. The next morn they lay long in bed, as wearied with the toil of unaccustomed travel, but as soon as they got up Aliena resolved there to set up her rest, and by the help of Corydon swapped[3] a bargain with his landlord, and so became mistress of the farm and the flock, herself putting on the attire of a shepherdess and Ganymede of a young swain, every day leading forth her flocks with such delight that she held her exile happy, and thought no content to the bliss of a country cottage. Leaving her thus famous amongst the shepherds of Arden, again to Saladyn.

When Saladyn had a long while concealed a secret resolution of revenge, and could no longer hide fire in the flax, nor oil in the flame (for envy is like lightning, that will appear in the darkest fog), it chanced on a morning very early, he called up certain of his servants and went with them to the chamber of Rosader, which being open, he entered with his crew, and surprised his brother being asleep and bound him in fetters, and in the midst of his hall chained him to a post. Rosader, amazed at this strange chance, began to reason with his brother about the cause of this sudden extremity, wherein he had wronged and what fault he had committed

---

1. lapidary] One concerned with stones.
2. Narcissus] Greek myth; beautiful youth loved by the nymph Echo. Narcissus rejects her and is punished by Aphrodite, who makes him fall in love with his own image. His fruitless attempts to approach his reflection led to his despair and death.
3. swapped] Concluded ('swapt' in Q2, 'swept' in Q1).

worthy so sharp a penance. Saladyn answered him only with a look of disdain and went his way, leaving poor Rosader in a deep perplexity, who (thus abused) fell into sundry passions, but no means of relief could be had, whereupon for anger he grew into a discontented melancholy, in which humour he continued two or three days without meat, insomuch that seeing his brother would give him no food, he fell into despair of his life. Which Adam Spencer, the old servant of Sir John of Bordeaux, seeing, touched with the duty and love he ought to his old master, felt a remorse in his conscience of his son's mishap, and therefore, although Saladyn had given a general charge to his servants that none of them upon pain of death should give either meat or drink to Rosader, yet Adam Spencer in the night arose secretly and brought him such victuals as he could provide, and unlocked him and set him at liberty. After Rosader had well feasted himself and felt he was loose, straight his thoughts aimed at revenge, and now, all being asleep, he would have quit Saladyn with the method of his own mischief. But Adam Spencer persuaded him to the contrary with these reasons: 'Sir,' quoth he, 'be content, for this night go again into your old fetters, so shall you try the faith of friends and save the life of an old servant. Tomorrow hath your brother invited all your kindred and allies to a solemn breakfast, only to see you, telling them all that you are mad and fain to be tied to a post. As soon as they come, make complaint to them of the abuse proffered you by Saladyn. If they redress you, why so, but if they pass over your plaints *sicco pede*,[1] and hold with the violence of your brother before your innocence, then thus: I will leave you unlocked that you may break out at your pleasure, and at the end of the hall shall you see stand a couple of good poleaxes, one for you and another for me. When I give you a wink, shake off your chains and let us play the men and make havoc amongst them, drive them out of the house and maintain possession by force of arms till the king hath made a redress of your abuses.' These words of Adam Spencer so persuaded Rosader that he went to the place of his punishment and stood there while the next morning. About the time appointed, came all the guests bidden by Saladyn, whom he entreated with courteous and curious entertainment, as they all perceived their welcome to be great. The tables in the hall where Rosader was tied were covered, and Saladyn bringing in his guests together showed them where his brother was bound, and was enchained as a man lunatic. Rosader made reply, and with some invectives made complaints of the wrongs proffered him by Saladyn, desiring they would in pity seek some means for his relief. But in vain, they had stopped their ears with Ulysses, that were his words never so forcible, he breathed only his

---

1. *sicco pede*] Dry-foot; carelessly.

passions into the wind. They, careless, sat down with Saladyn to dinner, being very frolic and pleasant, washing their heads well with wine. At last, when the fume of the grape had entered peal-meal[1] into their brains, they began in satirical speeches to rail against Rosader, which Adam Spencer no longer brooking, gave the sign, and Rosader shaking off his chains got a poleaxe in his hand and flew amongst them with such violence and fury that he hurt many, slew some, and drove his brother and all the rest quite out of the house. Seeing the coast clear, he shut the doors, and being sore anhungered and seeing such good victuals, he sat him down with Adam Spencer and such good fellows as he knew were honest men, and there feasted themselves with such provision as Saladyn had prepared for his friends. After they had taken their repast Rosader rampiered up the house, lest upon a sudden his brother should raise some crew of his tenants and surprise them unawares. But Saladyn took a contrary course and went to the sheriff of the shire and made complaint of Rosader, who giving credit to Saladyn, in a determined resolution to revenge the gentleman's wrongs, took with him five-and-twenty tall men, and made a vow either to break into the house and take Rosader or else to coop him in till he made him yield by famine. In this determination, gathering a crew together, he went forward to set Saladyn in his former estate. News of this was brought unto Rosader, who smiling at the cowardice of his brother, brooked all the injuries of Fortune with patience, expecting the coming of the sheriff. As he walked upon the battlements of the house, he descried where Saladyn and he drew near with a troop of lusty gallants. At this he smiled and called up Adam Spencer, and showed him the envious treachery of his brother, and the folly of the sheriff to be so credulous. 'Now Adam,' quoth he, 'What shall I do? It rests for me either to yield up the house to my brother and seek a reconcilement, or else issue out and break through the company with courage, for cooped in like a coward I will not be. If I submit, ah Adam, I dishonour myself, and that is worse than death, for by such open disgraces the fame of men grows odious; if I issue out amongst them, Fortune may favour me, and I may escape with life; but suppose the worst, if I be slain, then my death shall be honourable to me, and so unequal a revenge infamous to Saladyn.' 'Why then, master, forward and fear not! Out amongst them, they be but faint-hearted losels,[2] and for Adam Spencer, if he die not at your foot, say he is a dastard.' These words cheered up so the heart of young Rosader that he thought himself sufficient for them all, and therefore prepared weapons for him and Adam Spencer, and were ready to entertain the sheriff; for no sooner came Saladyn and he to the

---

1.   peal-meal] Pell-mell.
2.   losels] Worthless people; scoundrels.

gates but Rosader unlooked-for leaped out and assailed them, wounded many of them, and caused the rest to give back, so that Adam and he broke through the prease[1] in despite of them all and took their way towards the forest of Arden. This repulse so set the sheriff's heart on fire to revenge that he straight raised all the country and made hue and cry after them. But Rosader and Adam, knowing full well the secret ways that led through the vineyards, stole away privily through the province of Bordeaux, and escaped safe to the forest of Arden. Being come thither, they were glad they had so good a harbour: but Fortune, who is like the chameleon, variable with every object and constant in nothing but inconstancy, thought to make them mirrors of her mutability, and therefore still crossed them thus contrarily. Thinking still to pass on by the byways to get to Lyons, they chanced on a path that led into the thick of the forest, where they wandered five or six days without meat, that they were almost famished, finding neither shepherd nor cottage to relieve them; and hunger growing on so extreme, Adam Spencer (being old) began first to faint, and sitting him down on a hill and looking about him espied where Rosader lay as feeble and as ill perplexed, which sight made him shed tears and to fall to these bitter terms:

Adam Spencer's Speech.

'Oh how the life of man may well be compared to the state of the ocean seas, that for every calm hath a thousand storms, resembling the rose tree, that for a few fair flowers, hath a multitude of sharp prickles! All our pleasures end in pain and our highest delights are crossed with deepest discontents. The joys of man, as they are few, so are they momentary, scarce ripe before they are rotten, and withering in the blossom, either parched with the heat of envy or fortune. Fortune, O inconstant friend, that in all thy deeds are froward and fickle, delighting in the poverty of the lowest and the overthrow of the highest to decipher thy inconstancy. Thou standest upon a globe, and thy wings are plumed with Time's feathers that thou mayest ever be restless. Thou art double-faced like Janus,[2] carrying frowns in the one to threaten and smiles in the other to betray. Thou profferest an eel and performest a scorpion, and where thy greatest favours be there is the fear of the extremest misfortunes, so variable are all thy actions. But why, Adam, dost thou exclaim against Fortune? She laughs at the plaints of the distressed, and there is nothing more pleasing unto her than to hear fools boast in her fading allurements, or sorrowful men to discover the sour of their passions. Glut her not, Adam, then with content,

---

1. prease] Press, crowd.
2. Janus] The two-headed Roman God of doors and entrances.

but thwart her with brooking all mishaps with patience. For there is no greater check to the pride of Fortune than with a resolute courage to pass over her crosses without care. Thou art old, Adam, and thy hairs wax white; the palm tree is already full of blooms, and in the furrows of thy face appears the calendars of death. Wert thou blessed by Fortune thy years could not be many, nor the date of thy life long; then sith Nature must have her due, what is it for thee to resign her debt a little before the day. Ah, it is not this which grieveth me, nor do I care what mishaps Fortune can wage against me, but the sight of Rosader that galleth unto the quick. When I remember the worships of his house, the honour of his fathers, and the virtues of himself, then do I say that Fortune and the fates are most injurious to censure so hard extremes against a youth of so great hope. O Rosader, thou art in the flower of thine age and in the pride of thy years, buxom and full of May. Nature hath prodigally enriched thee with her favours and virtue made thee the mirror of her excellence, and now, through the decree of the unjust stars, to have all these good parts nipped in the blade and blemished by the inconstancy of Fortune! Ah Rosader, could I help thee, my grief were the less, and happy should my death be if it might be the beginning of thy relief, but seeing we perish both in one extreme it is a double sorrow. What shall I do? Prevent the sight of his further misfortune with a present dispatch of mine own life? Ah, despair is a merciless sin!'

As he was ready to go forward in his passion, he looked earnestly on Rosader, and seeing him change colour, he rose up and went to him, and holding his temples said, 'What cheer, master? Though all fail, let not the heart faint; the courage of a man is showed in the resolution of his death.' At those words Rosader lifted up his eye, and looking on Adam Spencer began to weep. 'Ah Adam,' quoth he, 'I sorrow not to die, but I grieve at the manner of my death. Might I with my lance encounter the enemy and so die in the field, it were honour and content; might I, Adam, combat with some wild beast and perish as his prey, I were satisfied; but to die with hunger, O Adam, it is the extremest of all extremes!' 'Master,' quoth he, 'you see we are both in one predicament, and long I cannot live without meat; seeing therefore we can find no food, let the death of the one preserve the life of the other. I am old and overworn with age, you are young and are the hope of many honours. Let me then die, I will presently cut my veins, and, master, with the warm blood relieve your fainting spirits: suck on that till I end and you be comforted.' With that Adam Spencer was ready to pull out his knife, when Rosader full of courage (though very faint) rose up and wished Adam Spencer to sit there till his return: 'For my mind gives me,' quoth he, 'I shall bring thee meat.' With that, like a madman he rose up and ranged up and down the woods, seeking to encounter some wild beast with his rapier, that either he might carry his friend Adam food, or else pledge his life in pawn of his loyalty. It chanced that day that Gerismond, the lawful king of France banished by Torismond, who with a lusty crew of outlaws lived in that forest, that day in honour of his birth made a feast to all his bold yeomen and frolicked it with store of wine and venison, sitting all at a long table under the shadow of lemon trees. To that place by chance Fortune conducted Rosader, who seeing such a crew of brave men having store of that for want of which he and Adam perished, he stepped boldly to the board's end and saluted the company thus:

'Whatsoever thou be that art master of these lusty squires, I salute thee as graciously as a man in extreme distress may. Know that I and a fellow-friend of mine are here famished in the forest for want of food; perish we must unless relieved by thy favours. Therefore if thou be a gentleman, give meat to men, and to such men as are every way worthy of life. Let the proudest squire that sits at thy table rise and encounter with me in any honourable point of activity whatsoever, and if he and thou prove me not a man, send me away comfortless. If thou refuse this, as a niggard of thy cates, I will have amongst you with my sword, for rather will I die valiantly than perish with so cowardly an extreme.' Gerismond looking him earnestly in the face, and seeing so proper a gentleman in so bitter a passion, was moved with so great pity, that rising from the table, he took him by the hand and bad him welcome, willing him to sit down in his place and in his room not only to eat his fill, but be lord of the feast. 'Gramercy sir,' quoth Rosader, 'but I have a feeble friend that lies hereby famished almost for food, aged and therefore less able to abide the extremity of hunger than myself, and dishonour it were for me to taste one crumb before I made him partner of my fortunes. Therefore I will run and fetch him, and then I will gratefully accept of your proffer.' Away hies Rosader to Adam Spencer and tells him the news, who was glad of so happy fortune but so feeble he was that he could not go, whereupon Rosader got him up on his back and brought him to the place. Which when Gerismond and his men saw, they greatly applauded their league of friendship, and Rosader, having Gerismond's place assigned to him, would not sit there himself but set down Adam Spencer. Well, to be short, those hungry squires fell to their victuals, and feasted themselves with good delicates and great store of wine. As soon as they had taken their repast, Gerismond (desirous to hear what hard fortune drove them into those bitter extremes) requested Rosader to discourse, if it were not any way prejudicial unto him, the cause of his travel. Rosader, desirous any way to satisfy the courtesy of his favourable host, first beginning his exordium[1] with a volley of sighs and a few lukewarm

---

1. exordium] The introductory part of a discourse, treatise.

tears, prosecuted his discourse and told him from point to point all his fortunes; how he was the youngest son of Sir John of Bordeaux, his name Rosader, how his brother sundry times had wronged him, and lastly how, for beating the sheriff and hurting his men, he fled. 'And this old man,' quoth he, 'whom I so much love and honour, is surnamed Adam Spencer, an old servant of my father's, and one that for his love never failed me in all my misfortunes.' When Gerismond heard this, he fell on the neck of Rosader, and next discoursing unto him how he was Gerismond their lawful king exiled by Torismond, what familiarity had ever been betwixt his father, Sir John of Bordeaux, and him, how faithful a subject he lived, and how honourable he died, promising for his sake to give both him and his friend such courteous entertainment as his present estate could minister, and upon this made him one of his foresters. Rosader, seeing it was the king, craved pardon for his boldness in that he did not do him due reverence, and humbly gave him thanks for his favourable courtesy. Gerismond, not satisfied yet with news, began to enquire if he had been lately in the court of Torismond, and whether he had seen his daughter Rosalynd, or no? At this Rosader fetched a deep sigh, and shedding many tears could not answer; yet at last, gathering his spirits together, he revealed unto the king how Rosalynd was banished, and how there was such sympathy of affections between Alinda and her that she chose rather to be partaker of her exile than to part fellowship, whereupon the unnatural king banished them both, and now they are wandered none knows whither, neither could any learn since their departure the place of their abode. This news drove the king into a great melancholy, that presently he arose from all the company and went into his privy chamber, so secret as the harbour of the woods would allow him. The company was all dashed at these tidings, and Rosader and Adam Spencer having such opportunity, went to take their rest. Where we leave them, and return again to Torismond. The flight of Rosader came to the ears of Torismond, who hearing that Saladyn was sole heir of the lands of Sir John of Bordeaux, desirous to possess such fair revenues, found just occasion to quarrel with Saladyn about the wrongs he proffered to his brother, and therefore, dispatching a herehault,[1] he sent for Saladyn in all post-haste. Who marvelling what the matter should be, began to examine his own conscience, wherein he had offended his Highness, but emboldened with his innocence he boldly went with the herehault unto the court. Where as soon as he came, he was not admitted into the presence of the king, but presently sent to prison. This greatly amazed Saladyn, chiefly in that the jailer had a straight charge over him to see that he should be close prisoner. Many passionate

---

1. herehault] Herald.

thoughts came in his head till at last he began to fall into consideration of his former follies, and to meditate with himself. Leaning his head on his hand and his elbow on his knee, full of sorrow, grief and disquieted passions, he resolved into these terms:

Saladyn's Complaint.

'Unhappy Saladyn, whom folly hath led to these misfortunes, and wanton desires wrapped within the labyrinth of these calamities! Are not the heavens doomers of men's deeds, and holds not God a balance in his fist, to reward with favour and revenge with justice? O Saladyn, the faults of thy youth, as they were fond so were they foul, and not only discovering little nurture, but blemishing the excellence of nature. Whelps of one litter are ever most loving, and brothers that are sons of one father should live in friendship without jar. O Saladyn, so it should be, but thou hast with the deer fed against the wind, with the crab strove against the stream, and sought to pervert nature by unkindness. Rosader's wrongs, the wrongs of Rosader, Saladyn, cries for revenge; his youth pleads to God to inflict some penance upon thee, his virtues are pleas that enforce writs of displeasure to cross thee, thou hast highly abused thy kind and natural brother, and the heavens cannot spare to quite thee with punishment. There is no sting to the worm of conscience, no hell to a mind touched with guilt. Every wrong I offered him, called now to remembrance, wringeth a drop of blood from my heart, every bad look, every frown pincheth me at the quick, and says "Saladyn thou hast sinned against Rosader." Be penitent, and assign thy self some penance to discover thy sorrow and pacify his wrath.'

In the depth of his passion, he was sent for to the king, who with a look that threatened death, entertained him and demanded of him where his brother was. Saladyn made answer, that upon some riot made against the sheriff of the shire, he was fled from Bordeaux, but he knew not whither. 'Nay villain,' quoth he, 'I have heard of the wrongs thou hast proffered thy brother since the death of thy father, and by thy means have I lost a most brave and resolute chevalier. Therefore, in justice to punish thee, I spare thy life for thy father's sake, but banish thee for ever from the court and country of France; and see thy departure be within ten days, else trust me thou shalt lose thy head.' And with that the king flew away in a rage and left poor Saladyn greatly perplexed. Who grieving at his exile, yet determined to bear it with patience, and in penance of his former follies to travel abroad in every coast till he had found out his brother Rosader. With whom now I begin.

Rosader, being thus preferred to the place of a forester by Gerismond, rooted out the remembrance of his brother's unkindness by continual exercise, traversing the groves and wild forests, partly to hear the melody of the sweet birds which recorded,[1] and partly to show his diligent endeavour in his master's behalf. Yet whatsoever he did, or howsoever he walked, the lively image of Rosalynd remained in memory. On her sweet perfections he fed his thoughts, proving himself like the eagle a true-born bird, since as the one is known by beholding the sun, so was he by regarding excellent beauty. One day among the rest, finding a fit opportunity and place convenient, desirous to discover his woes to the woods, he engraved with his knife on the bark of a myrtle tree this pretty estimate of his mistress' perfection:

Sonetta.

Of all chaste birds the Phoenix doth excel,
Of all strong beasts the lion bears the bell,
Of all sweet flowers the rose doth sweetest smell,
Of all fair maids my Rosalynd is fairest.

Of all pure metals gold is only purest,
Of all high trees the pine hath highest crest,
Of all soft sweets I like my mistress' breast,
Of all chaste thoughts my mistress' thoughts are rarest.

Of all proud birds the eagle pleaseth Jove,
Of pretty fowls kind Venus likes the dove,
Of trees Minerva doth the olive love,
Of all sweet nymphs I honour Rosalynd.

Of all her gifts her wisdom pleaseth most,
Of all her graces virtue she doth boast:
For all these gifts my life and joy is lost,
If Rosalynd prove cruel and unkind.

In these and such like passions Rosader did every day eternize the name of his Rosalynd, and this day especially, when Aliena and Ganymede (enforced by the heat of the sun to seek for shelter), by good fortune arrived in that place where this amorous forester registered his melancholy passions. They saw the sudden change of his looks, his folded arms, his passionate sighs; they heard him often abruptly call on Rosalynd, who, poor soul, was as hotly burned as himself, but that she shrouded her pains

---

1.   recorded] Sang.

in the cinders of honourable modesty. Whereupon, guessing him to be in love, and according to the nature of their sex being pitiful in that behalf, they suddenly broke off his melancholy by their approach, and Ganymede shook him out of his dumps thus:

'What news, forester? Hast thou wounded some deer, and lost him in the fall? Care not man for so small a loss, thy fees was but the skin, the shoulder, and the horns: 'tis hunter's luck to aim fair and miss, and a woodman's fortune to strike and yet go without the game.'

'Thou art beyond the mark, Ganymede,' quoth Aliena, 'his passions are greater, and his sighs discover more loss. Perhaps in traversing these thickets he hath seen some beautiful nymph and is grown amorous.' 'It may be so,' quoth Ganymede, 'for here he hath newly engraven some sonnet: come and see the discourse of the forester's poems.' Reading the sonnet over and hearing him name Rosalynd, Aliena looked on Ganymede and laughed, and Ganymede, looking back on the forester and seeing it was Rosader, blushed; yet thinking to shroud all under her page's apparel, she boldly returned to Rosader and began thus:

'I pray thee tell me, forester, what is this Rosalynd for whom thou pinest away in such passions? Is she some nymph that waits upon Diana's train, whose chastity thou hast deciphered in such epithets? Or is she some shepherdess that haunts these plains, whose beauty hath so bewitched thy fancy, whose name thou shadowest in covert under the figure of Rosalynd, as Ovid did Julia under the name of Corinna? Or say me forsooth, is it that Rosalynd, of whom we shepherds have heard talk, she, forester, that is the daughter of Gerismond that once was king and now an outlaw in this forest of Arden?' At this Rosader fetched a deep sigh and said, 'It is she, O gentle swain, it is she; that saint it is whom I serve, that goddess at whose shrine I do bend all my devotions; the most fairest of all fairs, the phoenix of all that sex, and the purity of all earthly perfection.' 'And why, gentle forester, if she be so beautiful and thou so amorous, is there such a disagreement in thy thoughts? Haply she resembleth the rose that is sweet but full of prickles, or the serpent Regius[1] that hath scales as glorious as the sun, and a breath as infectious as the aconitum[2] is deadly? So thy Rosalynd may be most amiable and yet unkind, full of favour and yet froward, coy without wit and disdainful without reason.'

'O shepherd,' quoth Rosader, 'knewest thou her personage graced with the excellence of all perfection, being a harbour wherein the Graces shroud their virtues, thou wouldst not breathe out such blasphemy against the beauteous Rosalynd. She is a diamond, bright but not hard, yet of most

---

1. Regius] Type of serpent (compare King Cobra).
2. aconitum] Aconite or wolf's-bane, a poisonous plant.

chaste operation, a pearl so orient that it can be stained with no blemish, a rose without prickles, and a princess absolute as well in beauty as in virtue. But I, unhappy I, have let mine eye soar with the eagle against so bright a sun that I am quite blind. I have with Apollo enamoured myself of a Daphne,[1] not, as she, disdainful, but far more chaste than Daphne; I have with Ixion[2] laid my love on Juno, and shall, I fear, embrace nought but a cloud. Ah shepherd, I have reached at a star, my desires have mounted above my degree, and my thoughts above my fortunes. I, being a peasant, have ventured to gaze on a princess whose honours are too high to vouchsafe such base loves.'

'Why forester,' quoth Ganymede, 'comfort thyself, be blithe and frolic, man: Love sowseth[3] as low as she soareth high, Cupid shoots at a rag as soon as at a robe, and Venus' eye that was so curious sparkled favour on pole-footed[4] Vulcan.[5] Fear not, man, women's looks are not tied to dignity's feathers, nor make they curious esteem where the stone is found, but what is the virtue. Fear not, forester; faint heart never won fair lady. But where lives Rosalynd now – at the court?'

'Oh no,' quoth Rosader, 'she lives I know not where, and that is my sorrow; banished by Torismond, and that is my hell: for might I but find her sacred personage and plead before the bar of her pity the plaint of my passions, hope tells me she would grace me with some favour, and that would suffice as a recompense of all my former miseries.' 'Much have I heard of thy mistress' excellence, and I know, forester, thou canst describe her at the full, as one that hast surveyed all her parts with a curious eye; then do me that favour to tell me what her perfections be.' 'That I will,' quoth Rosader, 'for I glory to make all ears wonder at my mistress' excellence.' And with that he pulled a paper forth his bosom, wherein he read this:

Rosalynd's Description.

Like to the clear in highest sphere
Where all imperial glory shines,
Of selfsame colour is her hair
Whether unfolded or in twines:
  Heigh ho, fair Rosalynd.

---

1. Daphne] Greek myth; chaste nymph loved and pursued by Apollo.
2. Ixion] Greek myth: tried to seduce Jupiter's wife, Juno; Juno complained to Jupiter who, to trap Ixion, formed a cloud in the likeness of Juno and, by this cloud, Nephele, Ixion became the father of the centaurs.
3. sowseth] Swoops.
4. pole-footed] Club-footed.
5. Vulcan] Lame god of fire and metal-work, husband of Venus.

Her eyes are sapphires set in snow,
Refining heaven by every wink;
The gods do fear when as they glow,
And I do tremble when I think:
    Heigh ho, would she were mine.

Her cheeks are like the blushing cloud
That beautifies Aurora's face,
Or like the silver crimson shroud
That Phoebus' smiling looks doth grace:
    Heigh ho, fair Rosalynd.
Her lips are like two budded roses,
Whom ranks of lilies neighbour nigh,
Within which bounds she balm encloses,
Apt to entice a deity:
    Heigh ho, would she were mine.

Her neck like to a stately tower
Where Love himself imprisoned lies,
To watch for glances every hour
From her divine and sacred eyes:
    Heigh ho, fair Rosalynd.
Her paps [1] are centres of delight,
Her paps are orbs of heavenly frame,
Where Nature moulds the dew of light,
To feed perfection with the same:
    Heigh ho, would she were mine.

With orient pearl, with ruby red,
With marble white, with sapphire blue,
Her body every way is fed;
Yet soft in touch, and sweet in view:
    Heigh ho, fair Rosalynd.
Nature herself her shape admires,
The gods are wounded in her sight,
And Love forsakes his heavenly fires
And at her eyes his brand doth light:
    Heigh ho, would she were mine.

---

1.   paps] Teats or nipples of a woman's breast.

Then muse not, nymphs, though I bemoan
The absence of fair Rosalynd,
Since for her fair there is fairer none,
Nor for her virtues so divine:
    Heigh ho, fair Rosalynd;
    Heigh ho, my heart, would God that she were mine!

Periit, quia deperibat.[1]

'Believe me,' quoth Ganymede, 'either the forester is an exquisite painter, or Rosalynd fair[2] above wonder, so it makes me blush to hear how women should be so excellent, and pages so unperfect.'

Rosader beholding her earnestly, answered thus: 'Truly, gentle page, thou hast cause to complain thee wert thou the substance, but resembling the shadow, content thyself, for it is excellence enough to be like the excellence of Nature.' 'He hath answered you, Ganymede,' quoth Aliena, 'it is enough for pages to wait on beautiful ladies, and not to be beautiful themselves.' 'O mistress,' quoth Ganymede, 'hold you your peace, for you are partial. Who knows not, but that all women have desire to tie sovereignty to their petticoats and ascribe beauty to themselves, where if boys might put on their garments perhaps they would prove as comely; if not as comely, it may be more courteous. But tell me, forester' (and with that she turned to Rosader) 'under whom maintainest thou thy walk?' 'Gentle swain, under the king of outlaws,' said he, 'the unfortunate Gerismond, who having lost his kingdom, crowneth his thoughts with content, accounting it better to govern among poor men in peace than great men in danger.' 'But hast thou not,' said she, 'having so melancholy opportunities as this forest affordeth thee, written more sonnets in commendations of thy mistress?' 'I have, gentle swain,' quoth he, 'but they be not about me. Tomorrow by dawn of day, if your flocks feed in these pastures, I will bring them you, wherein you shall read my passions whilst I feel them. Judge my patience when you read it, till when I bid farewell.' So giving both Ganymede and Aliena a gentle good-night he resorted to his lodge, leaving Aliena and Ganymede to their prittle-prattle. 'So Ganymede,' said Aliena, the forester being gone, 'you are mightily beloved; men make ditties in your praise, spend sighs for your sake, make an idol of your beauty; believe me it grieves me not a little to see the poor man so pensive and you so pitiless.'

'Ah, Aliena,' quoth she, 'be not peremptory in your judgements; I hear Rosalynd praised as I am Ganymede, but were I Rosalynd I could answer

---

1. *Periit quia deperibat*] Latin: He perished because he was in despair.
2. fair] Q1's reading, but Q2's 'farre' is also possible.

the forester: If he mourn for love, there are medicines for love – Rosalynd cannot be fair and unkind. And so, madam, you see it is time to fold our flocks, or else Corydon will frown and say you will never prove good housewife.' With that they put their sheep into the cotes, and went home to her friend Corydon's cottage, Aliena as merry as might be that she was thus in the company of her Rosalynd; but she, poor soul, that had love her lodestar, and her thoughts set on fire with the flame of fancy, could take no rest, but being alone began to consider what passionate penance poor Rosader was enjoined to by love and fortune that at last she fell into this humour with herself:

Rosalynd passionate alone.

'Ah Rosalynd, how the Fates have set down in their synod to make thee unhappy, for when Fortune hath done her worst, then Love comes in to begin a new tragedy: she seeks to lodge her son in thine eyes and to kindle her fires in thy bosom. Beware, fond girl, he is an unruly guest to harbour, for cutting in by entreats, he will not be thrust out by force, and her fires are fed with such fuel as no water is able to quench. Seest thou not how Venus seeks to wrap thee in her labyrinth, wherein is pleasure at the entrance, but within, sorrows, cares, and discontent? She is a Siren, stop thine ears at her melody; and a basilisk,[1] shut thine eyes and gaze not at her lest thou perish. Thou art now placed in the country content, where are heavenly thoughts and mean desires. In those lawns where thy flocks feed Diana haunts: be as her nymphs, chaste and enemy to love, for there is no greater honour to a maid than to account of fancy as a mortal foe to their sex. Daphne, that bonny wench, was not turned into a bay tree as the poets feign, but for her chastity her fame was immortal, resembling the laurel that is ever green. Follow thou her steps, Rosalynd, and the rather, for that thou art an exile and banished from the court, whose distress, as it is appeased with patience, so it would be renewed with amorous passions. Have mind on thy forepassed fortunes, fear the worst, and entangle not thyself with present fancies, lest loving in haste thou repent thee at leisure. Ah, but yet, Rosalynd, it is Rosader that courts thee, one who as he is beautiful, so he is virtuous, and harboureth in his mind as many good qualities as his face is shadowed with gracious favours, and therefore, Rosalynd, stoop to love, lest being either too coy or too cruel, Venus wax wroth and plague thee with the reward of disdain.'

---

1. basilisk] In classical legend, a serpent that could kill by its breath or at a glance.

Rosalynd, thus passionate, was wakened from her dumps by Aliena, who said it was time to go to bed. Corydon swore that was true, for Charles' Wain[1] was risen in the north. Whereupon each taking leave of other, went to their rest all but the poor Rosalynd, who was so full of passions that she could not possess any content. Well, leaving her to her broken slumbers, expect what was performed by them the next morning.

The sun was no sooner stepped from the bed of Aurora, but Aliena was wakened by Ganymede, who restless all night had tossed in her passions, saying it was then time to go to the field to unfold their sheep. Aliena (that spied where the hare was by the hounds, and could see day at a little hole) thought to be pleasant with her Ganymede, and therefore replied thus: 'What, wanton! the sun is but new up, and as yet Iris' riches lie folded in the bosom of Flora; Phoebus hath not dried up the pearled dew, and so long Corydon hath taught me it is not fit to lead the sheep abroad, lest the dew being unwholesome, they get the rot. But now see I the old proverb true, he is in haste whom the devil drives, and where love pricks forward there is no worse death than delay. Ah my good page, is there fancy in thine eye, and passions in thy heart? What, hast thou wrapped love in thy looks and set all thy thoughts on fire by affection? I tell thee, it is a flame as hard to be quenched as that of Etna.[2] But nature must have her course, women's eyes have faculty attractive like the jet and retentive like the diamond, they dally in the delight of fair objects, till gazing on the panther's beautiful skin, repenting experience tell them he hath a devouring paunch.' 'Come on,' quoth Ganymede, 'this sermon of yours is but a subtlety to lie still a-bed, because either you think the morning cold, or else I being gone, you would steal a nap. This shift carries no palm, and therefore up and away. And for Love, let me alone; I'll whip him away with nettles and set disdain as a charm to withstand his forces, and therefore look to yourself, be not too bold, for Venus can make you bend, nor too coy, for Cupid hath a piercing dart that will make you cry *Peccavi*.'[3] 'And that is it,' quoth Aliena, 'that hath raised you so early this morning.' And with that she slipped on her petticoat and start up, and as soon as she had made her ready and taken her breakfast, away go these two with their bag and bottles to the field, in more pleasant content of mind than ever they were in the court of Torismond. They came no sooner nigh the folds, but they might see where their discontented forester was walking in his melancholy. As soon as Aliena saw him, she smiled, and said to Ganymede: 'Wipe your

---

1. Charles' Wain] The seven bright stars in Ursa Major; known also as the Plough.
2. Etna] Europe's highest active volcano, in Sicily.
3. *Peccavi*] Latin: I have erred.

eyes, sweeting, for yonder is your sweetheart this morning in deep prayers, no doubt to Venus, that she may make you as pitiful as he is passionate. Come on, Ganymede, I pray thee let's have a little sport with him.' 'Content,' quoth Ganymede, and with that, to waken him out of his deep *memento*, he began thus:

'Forester, good fortune to thy thoughts and ease to thy passions; what makes you so early abroad this morn? In contemplation, no doubt of your Rosalynd. Take heed, forester, step not too far, the ford may be deep and you slip over the shoes. I tell thee, flies have their spleen, the ants choler, the least hairs shadows, and the smallest loves great desires. 'Tis good, forester, to love, but not to overlove, lest in loving her that likes not thee, thou fold thyself in an endless labyrinth.' Rosader, seeing the fair shepherdess and her pretty swain, in whose company he felt the greatest ease of his care, he returned them a salute on this manner:

'Gentle shepherds, all hail, and as healthful be your flocks as you happy in content. Love is restless, and my bed is but the cell of my bane, in that there I find busy thoughts and broken slumbers. Here, although everywhere passionate, yet I brook love with more patience, in that every object feeds mine eye with variety of fancies; when I look on Flora's beauteous tapestry, chequered with the pride of all her treasure, I call to mind the fair face of Rosalynd, whose heavenly hue exceeds the rose and the lily in their highest excellence; the brightness of Phoebus' shine puts me in mind to think of the sparkling flames that flew from her eyes and set my heart first on fire; the sweet harmony of the birds puts me in remembrance of the rare melody of her voice, which like the Siren enchanteth the ears of the hearer. Thus in contemplation I salve my sorrows, with applying the perfection of every object to the excellence of her qualities.'

'She is much beholding unto you,' quoth Aliena, 'and so much, that I have oft wished with myself that if I should ever prove as amorous as Oenone,[1] I might find as faithful a Paris as yourself.'

'How say you by this item, forester,' quoth Ganymede, 'the fair shepherdess favours you, who is mistress of so many flocks. Leave off, man, the supposition of Rosalynd's love, whenas watching at her you rove beyond the moon, and cast your looks upon my mistress, who no doubt is as fair, though not so royal. One bird in the hand is worth two in the wood; better possess the love of Aliena than catch frivolously at the shadow of Rosalynd.'

'I'll tell thee boy,' quoth Rosader,[2] 'so is my fancy fixed on my Rosalynd

---

1. Oenone] Greek myth; nymph of Mount Ida near Troy who was loved by Paris before he knew that he was a Trojan prince.
2. Rosader] Greg's correction of the Quartos' 'Ganymede'.

that were thy mistress as fair as Leda[1] or Danae,[2] whom Jove courted in transformed shapes, mine eyes would not vouch to entertain their beauties, and so hath love locked me in her perfections that I had rather only contemplate in her beauties than absolutely possess the excellence of any other.' 'Venus is to blame, forester, if having so true a servant of you, she reward you not with Rosalynd, if Rosalynd were more fairer than herself. But leaving this prattle, now I'll put you in mind of your promise about those sonnets which you said were at home in your lodge.' 'I have them about me,' quoth Rosader, 'let us sit down, and then you shall hear what a poetical fury love will infuse into a man.' With that they sat down upon a green bank shadowed with fig trees, and Rosader, fetching a deep sigh, read them this sonnet:

Rosader's Sonnet.

In sorrow's cell I laid me down to sleep,
But waking woes were jealous of mine eyes,
They made them watch, and bend themselves to weep,
But weeping tears their want could not suffice:
      Yet since for her they wept who guides my heart,
      They weeping smile, and triumph in their smart.

Of these my tears a fountain fiercely springs,
Where Venus bains[3] herself incensed with love,
Where Cupid bowseth[4] his fair feathered wings;
But I behold what pains I must approve.
      Care drinks it dry: but when on her I think,
      Love makes me weep it full unto the brink.

Meanwhile my sighs yield truce unto my tears,
By them the wind increased and fiercely blow:
Yet when I sigh the flame more plain appears,
And by their force with greater power doth glow:
      Amidst these pains, all phoenix-like I thrive,
      Since love that yields me death may life revive.

Rosader en esperance.[5]

---

1. Leda] Greek myth; mother of Helen of Troy. Zeus approached her in the form of a swan.
2. Danae] Greek myth; daughter of Acrisius. An oracle foretold that Acrisius would be killed by his daughter's son and he therefore confined Danae in a bronze tower so that no man might approach her; but Jupiter descended on her in a shower of gold and she bore a son, Perseus.
3. bains] Bathes; from French baigner.   4. bowseth] Bathes.
5. Rosader en esperance] French: Rosader in hope.

'Now surely, forester,' quoth Aliena, 'when thou madest this sonnet thou wert in some amorous quandary, neither too fearful as despairing of thy mistress' favours, nor too gleesome as hoping in thy fortunes.' 'I can smile,' quoth Ganymede, 'at the sonnetos,[1] canzones,[2] madrigals, rounds[3] and roundelays that these pensive patients pour out when their eyes are more full of wantonness than their hearts of passions. Then, as the fishers put the sweetest bait to the fairest fish, so these Ovidians,[4] holding *Amo*[5] in their tongues when their thoughts come at haphazard, write that they be wrapped in an endless labyrinth of sorrow, when walking in the large lease of liberty, they only have their humours in their inkpot. If they find women so fond that they will with such painted lures come to their lust, then they triumph till they be full gorged with pleasures and then fly they away, like ramage[6] kites, to their own content, leaving the tame fool their mistress full of fancy, yet without ever a feather. If they miss (as dealing with some wary wanton that wants not such a one as themselves, but spies their subtlety) they end their amours with a few feigned sighs and so their excuse is, their mistress is cruel, and they smother passions with patience. Such, gentle forester, we may deem you to be, that rather pass away the time here in these woods with writing amorets than to be deeply enamoured, as you say, of your Rosalynd. If you be such a one, then I pray God, when you think your fortunes at the highest, and your desires to be most excellent, then that you may with Ixion embrace Juno in a cloud, and have nothing but a marble mistress to release your martyrdom. But if you be true and trusty, eye-pained and heart-sick, then accursed be Rosalynd if she prove cruel, for forester, I flatter not, thou art worthy of as fair as she.' Aliena spying the storm by the wind, smiled to see how Ganymede flew to the fist without any call, but Rosader who took him flat for a shepherd's swain made him this answer:

'Trust me, swain,' quoth Rosader, 'but my canzon[7] was written in no such humour, for mine eye and my heart are relatives, the one drawing fancy by sight, the other entertaining her by sorrow. If thou sawest my Rosalynd, with what beauties Nature hath favoured her, with what perfections the heavens hath graced her, with what qualities the gods have endued her,

---

1. sonnetos] Sonnets.
2. canzones] Originally in Italian or Provençal, a song, ballad, species of lyric, closely resembling the madrigal but less strict in style.
3. rounds] A kind of song sung by two or more persons, each taking up the strain in turn.
4. Ovidians] Alluding to the fashion at this time for amorous poetry in the style of Ovid.　　　　　　　　　　　　　　5. *Amo*] Latin: I love.
6. ramage] Untamed.　　　　　　　　　　7. canzon] A (love) song.

then wouldst say thou, there is none so fickle that could be fleeting unto her. If she had been Aeneas' Dido, had Venus and Juno both scolded him from Carthage, yet her excellence, despite of them, would have detained him at Tyre.[1] If Phyllis had been as beauteous, or Ariadne[2] as virtuous, or both as honourable and excellent as she, neither had the filbert tree sorrowed in the death of despairing Phyllis, nor the stars have been graced with Ariadne, but Demophoon and Theseus had been trusty to their paragons. I will tell thee, swain, if with a deep insight thou couldst pierce into the secret of my loves and see what deep impressions of her idea affection hath made in my heart, then wouldst thou confess I were passing passionate, and no less endued with admirable patience.' 'Why,' quoth Aliena, 'needs there patience in love?' 'Or else in nothing,' quoth Rosader, 'for it is a restless sore that hath no ease, a canker that still frets, a disease that taketh away all hope of sleep. If then so many sorrows, sudden joys, momentary pleasures, continual fears, daily griefs, and nightly woes be found in love, then is not he to be accounted patient that smothers all these passions with silence?' 'Thou speakest by experience,' quoth Ganymede, 'and therefore we hold all thy words for axioms – but is love such a lingering malady?' 'It is,' quoth he, 'either extreme or mean, according to the mind of the party that entertains it, for as the weeds grow longer untouched than the pretty flowers, and the flint lies safe in the quarry when the emerald is suffering the lapidary's tool, so mean men are freed from Venus' injuries when kings are environed with a labyrinth of her cares. The whiter the lawn is, the deeper is the mole; the more purer the chrysolite, the sooner stained; and such as have their hearts full of honour have their loves full of the greatest sorrows. But in whomsoever,' quoth Rosader, 'he fixeth his dart, he never leaveth to assault him till either he hath won him to folly or fancy, for as the moon never goes without the star Lunisequa, so a lover never goeth without the unrest of his thoughts. For proof you shall hear another fancy of my making.' 'Now do, gentle forester,' quoth Ganymede; and with that he read over this sonneto:

Rosader's second Sonneto.

Turn I my looks unto the skies,
Love with his arrows wounds mine eyes:

---

1. Tyre] Used for Carthage, presumably because Dido was daughter of the King of Tyre and her city a colony of the Phoenicians, whose major seaport was Tyre.
2. Phyllis … Ariadne] Respectively deserted by their faithless lovers Demophoon and Theseus in stories narrated in Ovid's *Heroides*.

If so I gaze upon the ground,
Love then in every flower is found.
Search I the shade to fly my pain,
He meets me in the shade again:
Wend I to walk in secret grove,
Even there I meet with sacred Love.
If so I bain me in the spring,
Even on the brink I hear him sing:
If so I meditate alone,
He will be partner of my moan.
If so I mourn, he weeps with me,
And where I am, there will he be.
Whenas I talk of Rosalynd,
The god from coyness waxeth kind,
And seems in selfsame flames to fry,
Because he loves as well as I.
Sweet Rosalynd, for pity rue,
For why, than Love I am more true:
He if he speed will quickly fly,
But in thy love I live and die.

'How like you this sonnet?' quoth Rosader. 'Marry,' quoth Ganymede, 'for the pen well, for the passion ill; for as I praise the one, I pity the other in that thou shouldst hunt after a cloud and love either without reward or regard.' ''Tis not her frowardness,' quoth Rosader, 'but my hard fortunes, whose destinies have crossed me with her absence; for did she feel my loves, she would not let me linger in these sorrows. Women, as they are fair, so they respect faith and estimate more, if they be honourable, the will than the wealth, having loyalty the object whereat they aim their fancies. But leaving off these interparleys,[1] you shall hear my last sonnetto and then you have heard all my poetry.' And with that he sighed out this:

Rosader's third Sonnet.

Of virtuous love myself may boast alone,
Since no suspect my service may attaint:
For perfect fair she is the only one,
Whom I esteem for my beloved saint:
    Thus for my faith I only bear the bell,[2]
    And for her fair she only doth excel.

---

1.   interparleys] Mutual talk, conversation.
2.   bear the bell] Carry off the prize.

Then let fond Petrarch shroud his Laura's praise,
And Tasso cease to publish his affect;
Since mine the faith confirmed at all assays,
And hers the fair, which all men do respect:
    My lines her fair, her fair my faith assures;
    Thus I by Love, and Love by me endures.

'Thus,' quoth Rosader, 'here is an end of my poems, but for all this no release of my passions, so that I resemble him that in the depth of his distress hath none but the echo to answer him.' Ganymede, pitying her Rosader, thinking to drive him out of this amorous melancholy, said that now the sun was in his meridional heat and that it was high noon, 'therefore we shepherds say 'tis time to go to dinner, for the sun and our stomachs are shepherd's dials. Therefore, forester, if thou wilt take such fare as comes out of our homely scrips,[1] welcome shall answer whatsoever thou wantest in delicates.' Aliena took the entertainment by the end, and told Rosader he should be her guest. He thanked them heartily, and sat with them down to dinner, where they had such cates as country state did allow them, sauced with such content, and such sweet prattle, as it seemed far more sweet than all their courtly junkets.

As soon as they had taken their repast, Rosader, giving them thanks for his good cheer, would have been gone; but Ganymede, that was loath to let him pass out of her presence, began thus: 'Nay forester,' quoth he, 'if thy business be not the greater, seeing thou sayest thou art so deeply in love, let me see how thou canst woo. I will represent Rosalynd, and thou shalt be as thou art, Rosader. See in some amorous eclogue, how if Rosalynd were present, how thou couldst court her; and while we sing of love, Aliena shall tune her pipe and play us melody.' 'Content,' quoth Rosader. And Aliena, she to show her willingness, drew forth a recorder and began to wind it. Then the loving forester began thus:

The wooing Eclogue betwixt Rosalynd and Rosader.

Rosader.
I pray thee, nymph, by all the working words,
By all the tears and sighs that lovers know,
Or what or thoughts or faltering tongue affords,
I crave for mine in ripping up my woe.
Sweet Rosalynd, my love – would God, my love –
My life – would God, my life – aye pity me!

---

1.   scrips] Small bags.

Thy lips are kind, and humble like the dove,
And but with beauty pity will not be.
Look on mine eyes made red with rueful tears,
From whence the rain of true remorse descendeth,
All pale in looks am I[1] though young in years,
And nought but love or death my days befriendeth.
Oh let no stormy rigour knit thy brows,
Which Love appointed for his mercy seat:
The tallest tree by Boreas'[2] breath it bows,
The iron yields with hammer, and to heat.
    O Rosalynd, then be thou pitiful,
    For Rosalynd is only beautiful.

Rosalynd.

Love's wantons arm their traitorous suits with tears,
With vows, with oaths, with looks, with showers of gold:
But when the fruit of their affects appears,
The simple heart by subtle sleights is sold.
Thus sucks the yielding ear the poisoned bait,
Thus feeds the heart upon his endless harms,
Thus glut the thoughts themselves on self-deceit,
Thus blind the eyes their sight by subtle charms.
The lovely looks, the sighs that storm so sore,
The dew of deep-dissembled doubleness:
These may attempt, but are of power no more
Where beauty leans to wit and soothfastness.
    O Rosader, then be thou witiful,
    For Rosalynd scorns foolish pitiful.

Rosader.

I pray thee, Rosalynd, by those sweet eyes
That stain the sun in shine, the morn in clear,
By those sweet cheeks where Love encamped lies
To kiss the roses of the springing year.
I tempt thee, Rosalynd, by ruthful plaints,
Not seasoned with deceit or fraudful guile,
But firm in pain, far more than tongue depaints,
Sweet nymph be kind, and grace me with a smile.

---

1.   am I] Greg's correction of Q1's 'and I'.
2.   Boreas] The North wind.

So may the heavens preserve from hurtful food
Thy harmless flocks, so may the summer yield
The pride of all her riches and her good,
To fat thy sheep, the citizens of field.
Oh, leave to arm thy lovely brows with scorn:
The birds their beak, the lion hath his tail,
And lovers nought but sighs and bitter mourn,
The spotless fort of fancy to assail.
     O Rosalynd, then be thou pitiful:
     For Rosalynd is only beautiful.

Rosalynd.
The hardened steel by fire is brought in frame;

Rosader.
And Rosalynd my love than any wool more softer;
And shall not sighs her tender heart inflame?

Rosalynd.
Were lovers true, maids would believe them ofter.

Rosader.
Truth and regard and honour guide my love.

Rosalynd.
Fain would I trust, but yet I dare not try.

Rosader.
O pity me, sweet nymph, and do but prove.

Rosalynd.
I would resist, but yet I know not why.

Rosader.
O Rosalynd, be kind, for times will change,
Thy looks ay nill be fair as now they be,
Thine age from beauty may thy looks estrange:
Ah, yield in time, sweet nymph, and pity me.

Rosalynd.
     O Rosalynd, thou must be pitiful.
     For Rosader is young and beautiful.

Rosader.

Oh, gain more great than kingdoms or a crown!

Rosalynd.

Oh, trust betrayed if Rosader abuse me.

Rosader.

First let the heavens conspire to pull me down,
And heaven and earth as abject quite refuse me.
Let sorrows stream about my hateful bower,
And restless horror hatch within my breast,
Let beauty's eye afflict me with a lour,
Let deep despair pursue me without rest,
Ere Rosalynd my loyalty disprove,
Ere Rosalynd accuse me for unkind.

Rosalynd.

Then Rosalynd will grace thee with her love,
Then Rosalynd will have thee still in mind.

Rosader.

Then let me triumph more than Tithon's[1] dear,
Since Rosalynd will Rosader respect:
Then let my face exile his sorry cheer,
And frolic in the comfort of affect;
          And say that Rosalynd is only pitiful,
          Since Rosalynd is only beautiful.

When thus they had finished their courting eclogue in such a familiar clause, Ganymede, as augur of some good fortunes to light upon their affections, began to be thus pleasant: 'How now, forester, have I not fitted your turn? Have I not played the woman handsomely, and showed myself as coy in grants as courteous in desires, and been as full of suspicion as men of flattery? And yet to salve all, jumped[2] I not all up with the sweet union of love? Did not Rosalynd content her Rosader?' The forester at this smiling, shook his head, and folding his arms made this merry reply:

'Truth, gentle swain, Rosader hath his Rosalynd, but as Ixion had Juno, who thinking to possess a goddess, only embraced a cloud. In these

---

1. Tithon] Tithonus: Greek myth; son of Laomedon, king of Troy; loved by
    the goddess Eos, who asked that he be made immortal but forgot to ask that
    he be made eternally young.   2. jumped] Concluded.

imaginary fruitions of fancy I resemble the birds that fed themselves with Zeuxis'[1] painted grapes, but they grew so lean with pecking at shadows that they were glad with Aesop's[2] cock to scrape for a barley kernel. So fareth it with me, who to feed myself with the hope of my mistress' favours, sooth myself in thy suits, and only in conceit reap a wished-for content: but if my food be no better than such amorous dreams, Venus at the year's end shall find me but a lean lover. Yet do I take these follies for high fortunes, and hope these feigned affections do divine some unfeigned end of ensuing fancies.' 'And thereupon,' quoth Aliena, 'I'll play the priest: from this day forth Ganymede shall call thee husband, and thou shalt call Ganymede wife, and so we'll have a marriage.' 'Content,' quoth Rosader, and laughed. 'Content,' quoth Ganymede, and changed as red as a rose. And so with a smile and a blush they made up this jesting match, that after proved to a marriage in earnest, Rosader full little thinking he had wooed and won his Rosalynd. But all was well; hope is a sweet string to harp on, and therefore let the forester awhile shape himself to his shadow and tarry Fortune's leisure till she may make a metamorphosis fit for his purpose. I digress – and therefore to Aliena, who said the wedding was not worth a pin unless there were some cheer, nor that bargain well made that was not stricken up with a cup of wine, and therefore she willed Ganymede to set out such cates as they had, and to draw out her bottle, charging the forester, as he had imagined his loves, so to conceit these cates to be a most sumptuous banquet, and to take a mazer[3] of wine and to drink to his Rosalynd, which Rosader did, and so they passed away the day in many pleasant devices. Till at last Aliena perceived time would tarry no man, and that the sun waxed very low, ready to set, which made her shorten their amorous prattle and end the banquet with a fresh carouse, which done, they all three rose and Aliena broke off thus:

'Now forester, Phoebus that all this while hath been partaker of our sports, seeing every woodsman more fortunate in his loves than he in his fancies, seeing thou hast won Rosalynd when he could not woo Daphne, hides his head for shame and bids us adieu in a cloud. Our sheep, they poor wantons, wander towards their folds, as taught by Nature their due times of rest, which tells us, forester, we must depart. Marry, though there were a marriage, yet I must carry this night the bride with me, and tomorrow morning if you meet us here, I'll promise to deliver her as good

---

1. Zeuxis] Greek artist, whose painted fruit was said to be so realistic that the birds tried to eat it.
2. Aesop] Greek author of fables in which animals are given human characters and used to satirise human emotions.
3. mazer] A bowl or drinking cup.

a maid as I find her.' 'Content,' quoth Rosader, ''tis enough for me in the night to dream on love, that in the day am so fond to dote on love, and so till tomorrow you to your folds, and I will to my lodge.' And thus the forester and they parted. He was no sooner gone but Aliena and Ganymede went and folded their flocks, and taking up their hooks, their bags, and their bottles, hied[1] homeward. By the way, Aliena to make the time seem short began to prattle with Ganymede thus: 'I have heard them say that what the Fates forepoint, that Fortune pricketh down with a period; that the stars are sticklers in Venus' court, and desire hangs at the heel of Destiny; if it be so, then by all probable conjectures this match will be a marriage, for if augurism[2] be authentical, or the divines' dooms principles, it cannot be but such a shadow portends the issue of a substance, for to that end did the gods force the conceit of this eclogue that they might discover the ensuing consent of your affections, so that ere it be long I hope in earnest to dance at your wedding.'

'Tush,' quoth Ganymede, 'all is not malt that is cast on the kiln; there goes more words to a bargain than one; love feels no footing in the air and fancy holds it slippery harbour to nestle in the tongue; the match is not yet so surely made but he may miss of his market; but if Fortune be his friend I will not be his foe: and so I pray you, gentle mistress Aliena, take it.' 'I take all things well,' quoth she, 'that is your content, and am glad Rosader is yours, for now I hope your thoughts will be at quiet, your eye that ever looked at love will now lend a glance on your lambs, and then they will prove more buxom and you more blithe, for the eyes of the master feeds the cattle.' As thus they were in chat, they spied old Corydon where he came plodding to meet them, who told them supper was ready, which news made them speed home. Where we leave them to the next morrow and return to Saladyn.

All this while did poor Saladyn, banished from Bordeaux and the court of France by Torismond, wander up and down in the forest of Arden, thinking to get to Lyons, and so travel through Germany into Italy, but the forest being full of by-paths, and he unskilful of the country coast, slipped out of the way, and chanced up into the desert, not far from the place where Gerismond was and his brother Rosader. Saladyn, weary with wandering up and down, and hungry with long fasting, finding a little cave by the side of a thicket, eating such fruit as the forest did afford, and contenting himself with such drink as Nature had provided and thirst made delicate, after his repast he fell in a dead sleep. As thus he lay, a hungry lion came hunting down the edge of the grove for prey, and

---

1. hied] Hie; to hasten, speed.
2. augurism] Augury; the practice of divining from certain portents.

espying Saladyn began to seize upon him, but seeing he lay still without any motion, he left to touch him (for that lions hate to prey on dead carcases): and yet desirous to have some food the lion lay down and watched to see if he would stir. While thus Saladyn slept secure, Fortune that was careful over her champion, began to smile, and brought it to so pass that Rosader, having stricken a deer that but lightly hurt fled through the thicket, came pacing down by the grove with a boar-spear in his hand in great haste. He spied where a man lay asleep, and a lion fast by him. Amazed at this sight, as he stood gazing his nose on the sudden bled, which made him conjecture it was some friend of his. Whereupon drawing more nigh, he might easily discern his visage, and perceived by his physiognomy that it was his brother Saladyn, which drove Rosader into a deep passion, as a man perplexed at the sight of so unexpected a chance, marvelling what should drive his brother to traverse those secret deserts without any company, in such distress and forlorn sort. But the present time craved no such doubting ambages,[1] for either he must resolve to hazard his life for his relief, or else steal away and leave him to the cruelty of the lion. In which doubt, he thus briefly debated with himself:

Rosader's Meditation.

'Now Rosader, Fortune that long hath whipped thee with nettles, means to salve thee with roses, and having crossed thee with many frowns, now she presents thee with the brightness of her favours. Thou that didst count thyself the most distressed of all men mayst account thyself now the most fortunate amongst men, if Fortune can make men happy or sweet revenge be wrapped in a pleasing content. Thou seest Saladyn thine enemy, the worker of thy misfortunes and the efficient cause of thine exile, subject to the cruelty of a merciless lion, brought into this misery by the gods, that they might seem just in revenging his rigour and thy injuries. Seest thou not how the stars are in a favourable aspect, the planets in some pleasing conjunction, the fates agreeable to thy thoughts, and the destinies performers of thy desires, in that Saladyn shall die and thou free of his blood, he receive meed for his amiss and thou erect his tomb with innocent hands. Now Rosader, shalt thou return to Bordeaux and enjoy thy possessions by birth and his revenues by inheritance, now mayst thou triumph in love and hang Fortune's altars with garlands. For when Rosalynd hears of thy wealth, it will make her love thee more willingly, for women's eyes are made of Chrisecoll,[2] that is ever unperfect unless

---

1. ambages] Circuitous, secret or tortuous thoughts.
2. Chrisecoll] Glossed in Cotgrave's *Dictionary* as 'gold-solder; Borax; green earth ... a hard and shining mineral congealed in mines.'

tempered with gold, and Jupiter soonest enjoyed Danae because he came to her in so rich a shower. Thus shall this lion, Rosader, end the life of a miserable man, and from distress raise thee to be most fortunate.' And with that, casting his boar-spear on his neck, away he began to trudge. But he had not stepped back two or three paces but a new motion struck him to the very heart, that resting his boar-spear against his breast, he fell into this passionate humour:

'Ah Rosader, wert thou the son of Sir John of Bordeaux, whose virtues exceeded his valour, and yet the most hardiest knight in all Europe? Should the honour of the father shine in the actions of the son, and wilt thou dishonour thy parentage in forgetting the nature of a gentleman? Did not thy father at his last gasp breathe out this golden principle: brothers' amity is like the drops of balsamum[1] that salveth the most dangerous sores? Did he make a large exhort unto concord, and wilt thou show thyself careless? O Rosader, what though Saladyn hath wronged thee and made thee live an exile in the forest, shall thy nature be so cruel, or thy nurture so crooked, or thy thoughts so savage, as to suffer so dismal a revenge? What, to let him be devoured by wild beasts? *Non sapit, qui non sibi sapit*[2] is fondly spoken in such bitter extremes. Lose not his life, Rosader, to win a world of treasure, for in having him thou hast a brother, and by hazarding for his life thou gettest a friend and reconcilest an enemy, and more honour shalt thou purchase by pleasuring a foe than revenging a thousand injuries.'

With that his brother began to stir and the lion to rouse himself, whereupon Rosader suddenly charged him with the boar-spear and wounded the lion very sore at the first stroke. The beast feeling himself to have a mortal hurt leapt at Rosader, and with his paws gave him a sore pinch on the breast, that he had almost fallen; yet as a man most valiant, in whom the sparks of Sir John of Bordeaux remained, he recovered himself and in short combat slew the lion, who at his death roared so loud that Saladyn awaked, and starting up was amazed at the sudden sight of so monstrous a beast lying[3] slain by him and so sweet a gentleman wounded. He presently, as he was of a ripe conceit, began to conjecture that the gentleman had slain him in his defence. Whereupon, as a man in a trance, he stood staring on them both a good while, not knowing his brother, being in that disguise. At last he burst into these terms:

---

1. balsamum] An aromatic, oily or resinous medicinal preparation for healing external wounds or pain.
2. *Non … sapit*] Latin: He is not wise who knows not himself. See p. 33 n. 2.
3. lying] Q2; Q1 has 'lie'.

'Sir, whatsoever thou be, as full of honour thou must needs be by the view of thy present valour, I perceive thou hast redressed my fortunes by thy courage, and saved my life with thine own loss, which ties me to be thine in all humble service. Thanks thou shalt have as thy due, and more thou canst not have, for my ability denies me to perform a deeper debt. But if anyway it please thee to command me, use me as far at the power of a poor gentleman may stretch.'

Rosader, seeing he was unknown to his brother, wondered to hear such courteous words from his crabbed nature, but glad of such reformed nurture he made this answer: 'I am, sir, whatsoever thou art, a forester and ranger of these walks, who, following my deer to the fall, was conducted hither by some assenting fate, that I might save thee and disparage myself. For coming into this place, I saw thee asleep and the lion watching thy awake, that at thy rising he might prey upon thy carcase. At the first sight I conjectured thee a gentleman (for all men's thoughts ought to be favourable in imagination) and I counted it the part of a resolute man to purchase a stranger's relief, though with the loss of his own blood, which I have performed, thou seest, to mine own prejudice. If therefore thou be a man of such worth as I value thee by thy exterior lineaments, make discourse unto me what is the cause of thy present fortunes. For by the furrows in thy face thou seemest to be crossed with her frowns, but whatsoever or howsoever, let me crave that favour to hear the tragic cause of thy estate.' Saladyn sitting down and fetching a deep sigh, began thus:

Saladyn's Discourse to Rosader unknown.

'Although the discourse of my fortunes be the renewing of my sorrows, and the rubbing of the scar will open a fresh wound, yet that I may not prove ungrateful to so courteous a gentleman, I will rather sit down and sigh out my estate than give any offence by smothering my grief with silence. Know therefore, sir, that I am of Bordeaux, and the son and heir of Sir John of Bordeaux, a man for his virtues and valour so famous that I cannot think but the fame of his honours hath reached farther than the knowledge of his personage. The unfortunate son of so fortunate a knight am I, my name Saladyn, who succeeding my father in possessions but not in qualities, having two brethren committed by my father at his death to my charge, with such golden principles of brotherly concord as might have pierced like the Siren's melody into any human ear. But I, with Ulysses, became deaf against his philosophical harmony, and made more value of profit than of virtue, esteeming gold sufficient honour, and wealth the fittest title for a gentleman's dignity. I set my middle brother to the university to be a scholar, counting it enough if he might pore on a book while I fed upon his revenues, and for the youngest, which was my father's joy, young Rosader—' and with that naming of Rosader, Saladyn sat him down and wept.

'Nay, forward man,' quoth the forester, 'tears are the unfittest salve that any man can apply for to cure sorrows, and therefore cease from such feminine follies as should drop out of a woman's eye to deceive, not out of a gentleman's look to discover his thoughts, and forward with thy discourse.'

'O sir,' quoth Saladyn, 'this Rosader that wrings tears from mine eyes, and blood from my heart, was like my father in exterior personage and in inward qualities, for in the prime of his years he aimed all his acts at honour, and coveted rather to die than to brook any injury unworthy a gentleman's credit. I, whom envy had made blind, and covetousness masked with the veil of self-love, seeing the palm tree grow straight, thought to suppress it being a twig, but Nature will have her course, the cedar will be tall, the diamond bright, the carbuncle [1] glistering, and virtue will shine though it be never so much obscured. For I kept Rosader as a slave, and used him as one of my servile hinds, until age grew on and a secret insight of my abuse entered into his mind, insomuch that he could not brook it, but coveted to have what his father left him, and to live of himself. To be short, sir, I repined at his fortunes, and he counterchecked [2] me not with ability but valour, until at last by my friends and aid of such as followed gold more than right or virtue, I banished him from Bordeaux, and he, poor gentleman, lives no man knows where, in some distressed discontent. The gods, not able to suffer such impiety unrevenged, so wrought that the king picked a causeless quarrel against me in hope to have my lands, and so hath exiled me out of France for ever. Thus, thus sir, am I the most miserable of all men, as having a blemish in my thoughts for the wrongs I proffered Rosader, and a touch in my estate to be thrown from my proper possessions by injustice. Passionate thus with many griefs, in penance of my former follies, I go thus pilgrim-like to seek out my brother that I may reconcile myself to him in all submission, and afterward wend to the Holy Land to end my years in as many virtues as I have spent my youth in wicked vanities.'

Rosader, hearing the resolution of his brother Saladyn, began to compassionate his sorrows, and not able to smother the sparks of nature with feigned secrecy, he burst into these loving speeches: 'Then know, Saladyn,' quoth he, 'that thou hast met with Rosader, who grieves as much to see thy distress as thyself to feel the burden of thy misery.' Saladyn, casting up his

---

1.   carbuncle] Name variously applied to precious stones of a red or fiery colour.
2.   counterchecked] Rebuked.

eye and noting well the physiognomy of the forester, knew that it was his brother Rosader, which made him so bash and blush at the first meeting that Rosader was fain to recomfort him, which he did in such sort that he showed how highly he held revenge in scorn. Much ado there was between these two brethren, Saladyn in craving pardon, and Rosader in forgiving and forgetting all former injuries, the one submiss,[1] the other courteous, Saladyn penitent and passionate, Rosader kind and loving, that at length Nature working an union of their thoughts, they earnestly embraced, and fell from matters of unkindness to talk of the country life, which Rosader so highly commended that his brother began to have a desire to taste of that homely content. In this humour Rosader conducted him to Gerismond's lodge and presented his brother to the king, discoursing the whole matter how all had happened betwixt them. The king looking upon Saladyn found him a man of a most beautiful personage, and saw in his face sufficient sparks of ensuing honours, gave him great entertainment, and glad of their friendly reconcilement, promised such favour as the poverty of his estate might afford, which Saladyn gratefully accepted. And so Gerismond fell to question of Torismond's life. Saladyn briefly discoursed unto him his injustice and tyrannies with such modesty, although he had wronged him, that Gerismond greatly praised the sparing speech of the young gentleman.

Many questions passed, but at last Gerismond began with a deep sigh to enquire if there were any news of the welfare of Alinda or his daughter Rosalynd? 'None, sir,' quoth Saladyn, 'for since their departure they were never heard of.' 'Injurious Fortune,' quoth the king, 'that to double the father's misery, wrongst the daughter with misfortunes!' And with that, surcharged with sorrows, he went into his cell and left Saladyn and Rosader, whom Rosader straight conducted to the sight of Adam Spencer. Who, seeing Saladyn in that estate, was in a brown study; but when he heard the whole matter, although he grieved for the exile of his master, yet he joyed that banishment had so reformed him that from a lascivious youth he was proved a virtuous gentleman. Looking a longer while, and seeing what familiarity past between them and what favours were interchanged with brotherly affection, he said thus: 'Aye, marry, thus should it be; this was the concord that old Sir John of Bordeaux wished betwixt you. Now fulfil you those precepts he breathed out at his death, and in observing them look to live fortunate and die honourable.' 'Well said, Adam Spencer,' quoth Rosader, 'but hast any victuals in store for us?' 'A piece of a red deer,' quoth he, 'and a bottle of wine.' ''Tis forester's fare, brother,' quoth Rosader, and so they sat down and fell to their cates.

---

1. submiss] Submissive.

As soon as they had taken their repast, and had well dined, Rosader took his brother Saladyn by the hand and showed him the pleasures of the forest, and what content they enjoyed in that mean estate. Thus for two or three days he walked up and down with his brother, to show him all the commodities that belonged to his walk. In which time he was missed of his Ganymede, who mused greatly, with Aliena, what should become of their forester. Somewhile they thought he had taken some word unkindly and had taken the pet,[1] then they imagined some new love had withdrawn his fancy, or haply that he was sick, or detained by some great business of Gerismond's, or that he had made a reconcilement with his brother and so returned to Bordeaux. These conjectures did they cast in their heads, but especially Ganymede, who, having love in her heart, proved restless and half without patience that Rosader wronged her with so long absence; for Love measures every minute, and thinks hours to be days, and days to be months, till they feed their eyes with the sight of their desired object. Thus perplexed lived poor Ganymede, while on a day sitting with Aliena in a great dump, she cast up her eye and saw where Rosader came pacing towards them with his forest bill[2] on his neck. At that sight her colour changed and she said to Aliena: 'See, mistress, where our jolly forester comes.' 'And you are not a little glad thereof,' quoth Aliena, 'your nose bewrays what porridge you love, the wind cannot be tied within his quarter, the sun shadowed with a veil, oil hidden in water, nor love kept out of a woman's looks – but no more of that, *Lupus est in fabula*.'[3] As soon as Rosader was come within the reach of her tongue's end, Aliena began thus: 'Why how now, gentle forester, what wind hath kept you from hence, that being so newly married, you have no more care of your Rosalynd but to absent yourself so many days? Are these the passions you painted out so in your sonnets and roundelays? I see well hot love is soon cold, and that the fancy of men is like to a loose feather that wandereth in the air with the blast of every wind.' 'You are deceived, mistress,' quoth Rosader, ''twas a copy of unkindness that kept me hence, in that, I being married, you carried away the bride; but if I have given any occasion of offence by absenting myself these three days, I humbly sue for pardon, which you must grant of course, in that the fault is so friendly confessed with penance. But to tell you the truth, fair mistress and my good Rosalynd, my eldest brother, by the injury of Torismond, is banished from Bordeaux, and by chance he and I met in the forest.' And here Rosader discoursed

---

1. taken the pet] From the phrase 'to take the pet'; to take offence and become ill-humoured or sulky.
2. forest bill] Woodman's billhook, used for pruning, cutting brushwood etc.
3. *Lupus est in fabula*] Latin: Speak of the wolf and he will appear.

unto them what had happened betwixt them, which reconcilement made them glad, especially Ganymede. But Aliena, hearing of the tyranny of her father, grieved inwardly, and yet smothered all things with such secrecy that the concealing was more sorrow than the conceit; yet that her estate might be hid still, she made fair weather of it, and so let all pass.

Fortune, that saw how these parties valued not her deity, but held her power in scorn, thought to have a bout with them, and brought the matter to pass thus. Certain rascals that lived by prowling in the forest, who for fear of the provost marshal[1] had caves in the groves and thickets to shroud themselves from his trains, hearing of the beauty of this fair shepherdess Aliena, thought to steal her away and to give her to the king for a present, hoping, because the king was a great lecher, by such a gift to purchase all their pardons, and therefore came to take her and her page away. Thus resolved, while Aliena and Ganymede were in this sad talk, they came rushing in and laid violent hands upon Aliena and her page, which made them cry out to Rosader, who having the valour of his father stamped in his heart, thought rather to die in defence of his friends than any way be touched with the least blemish of dishonour, and therefore dealt such blows amongst them with his weapons as he did witness well upon their carcases that he was no coward. But as *Ne Hercules quidem contra duos*,[2] so Rosader could not resist a multitude, having none to back him, so that he was not only rebated,[3] but sore wounded, and Aliena and Ganymede had been quite carried away by these rascals had not Fortune (that meant to turn her frown into a favour) brought Saladyn that way by chance, who wandering to find out his brother's walk, encountered this crew, and seeing not only a shepherdess and her boy forced, but his brother wounded, he heaved up a forest bill he had on his neck and the first he struck had never after more need of the physician, redoubling his blows with such courage that the slaves were amazed at his valour.

Rosader, espying his brother so fortunately arrived, and seeing how valiantly he behaved himself, though sore wounded, rushed amongst them and laid on such load that some of the crew were slain and the rest fled, leaving Aliena and Ganymede in the possession of Rosader and Saladyn.

Aliena after she had breathed a while and was come to herself from this fear, looked about her and saw where Ganymede was busy dressing up the wounds of the forester, but she cast her eye upon this courteous champion that had made so hot a rescue, and that with such affection that she began to measure every part of him with favour, and in herself to commend his

---

1. provost marshal] Law-enforcement officer.
2. *Ne … duos*] Latin: Not even Hercules can win against two.
3. rebated] Beaten back.

personage and his virtue, holding him for a resolute man that durst assail such a troop of unbridled villains. At last, gathering her spirits together she returned him these thanks:

'Gentle sir, whatsoever you be that have adventured your flesh to relieve our fortunes, as we hold you valiant, so we esteem you courteous, and to have as many hidden virtues as you have manifest resolutions. We poor shepherds have no wealth but our flocks, and therefore can we not make requital with any great treasures, but our recompense is thanks, and our rewards to our friends without feigning. For ransom, therefore, of this our rescue, you must content yourself to take such a kind gramercy as a poor shepherdess and her page may give, with promise, in what we may, never to prove ungrateful. For this gentleman that is hurt, young Rosader, he is our good neighbour and familiar acquaintance; we'll pay him with smiles and feed him with love-looks, and though he be never the fatter at the year's end, yet we'll so hamper him that he shall hold himself satisfied.'

Saladyn, hearing this shepherdess speak so wisely, began more narrowly to pry into her perfection and to survey all her lineaments with a curious insight, so long dallying in the flame of her beauty that, to his cost, he found her to be most excellent. For Love that lurked in all these broils to have a blow or two, seeing the parties at the gaze, encountered them both with such a veny [1] that the stroke pierced to the heart so deep as it could never after be rased out. At last, after he had looked so long, till Aliena waxed red, he returned her this answer:

'Fair shepherdess, if Fortune graced me with such good hap as to do you any favour, I hold myself as contented as if I had gotten a great conquest, for the relief of distressed women is the special point that gentlemen are tied unto by honour. Seeing then my hazard to rescue your harms was rather duty than courtesy, thanks is more than belongs to the requital of such a favour. But lest I might seem either too coy or too careless of a gentlewoman's proffer, I will take your kind gramercy for a recompense.' All this while that he spoke, Ganymede looked earnestly upon him and said: 'Truly Rosader, this gentleman favours you much in the feature of your face.' 'No marvel,' quoth he, 'gentle swain, for 'tis my eldest brother Saladyn.' 'Your brother?' quoth Aliena, and with that she blushed. 'He is the more welcome, and I hold myself the more his debtor, and for that he hath in my behalf done such a piece of service, if it please him to do me that honour, I will call him servant and he shall call me mistress.' 'Content, sweet mistress,' quoth Saladyn, 'and when I forget to call you so, I will be unmindful of mine own self.' 'Away with these quirks and quiddities of love,' quoth Rosader, 'and give me some drink, for I am passing thirsty, and

---

1. veny] A hit or thrust in fencing.

then will I home, for my wounds bleed sore, and I will have them dressed.' Ganymede had tears in her eyes and passions in her heart to see her Rosader so pained, and therefore stepped hastily to the bottle, and filling out some wine in a mazer, she spiced it with such comfortable drugs as she had about her and gave it him, which did comfort Rosader, that rising, with the help of his brother, he took his leave of them and went to his lodge. Ganymede, as soon as they were out of sight, led his flocks down to a vale and there, under the shadow of a beech tree, sat down and began to mourn the misfortunes of her sweetheart.

And Aliena, as a woman passing discontent, severing herself from her Ganymede, sitting under a lemon tree, began to sigh out the passions of her new love, and to meditate with herself on this manner:

Aliena's Meditation.

'Ay me, now I see, and sorrowing sigh to see, that Diana's laurels are harbours for Venus' doves, that there trace as well through the lawns wantons as chaste ones, that Calisto,[1] be she never so chary,[2] will cast one amorous eye at courting Jove, that Diana herself will change her shape, but she will honour Love in a shadow, that maidens' eyes be they as hard as diamonds, yet Cupid hath drugs to make them more pliable than wax. See Alinda, how Fortune and Love have interleagued themselves to be thy foes, and to make thee their subject, or else an abject, have inveigled thy sight with a most beautiful object. A-late thou didst hold Venus for a giglot,[3] not a goddess, and now thou shalt be forced to sue suppliant to her Deity. Cupid was a boy and blind, but, alas, his eye had aim enough to pierce thee to the heart. While I lived in the court I held love in contempt, and in high seats I had small desires. I knew not affection while I lived in dignity, nor could Venus countercheck me as long as my fortune was majesty and my thoughts honour: and shall I now be high in desires when I am made low by destiny?

'I have heard them say, that Love looks not at low cottages, that Venus jets in robes not in rags, that Cupid flies so high that he scorns to touch poverty with his heel. Tush Alinda, these are but old wives' tales, and neither authentical precepts nor infallible principles, for experience tells thee that peasants have their passions as well as princes, that swains as they have their labours, so they have their amours, and Love lurks as soon about a sheepcote as a palace.

---

1. Calisto] Greek myth; a nymph attendant upon the goddess Artemis; loved by Zeus, who changed her into a bear to save her from the anger of his consort Hera.
2. chary] Careful, cautious.   3.   giglot] Originally a lewd, wanton woman.

'Ah Alinda, this day in avoiding a prejudice thou art fallen into a deeper mischief; being rescued from the robbers, thou art become captive to Saladyn – and what then? Women must love, or they must cease to live, and therefore did Nature frame them fair that they might be subjects to fancy. But perhaps Saladyn's eye is levelled upon a more seemlier saint. If it be so, bear thy passions with patience, say Love hath wronged thee that hath not wrung him, and if he be proud in contempt, be thou rich in content, and rather die than discover any desire, for there is nothing more precious in a woman than to conceal love and to die modest. He is the son and heir of Sir John of Bordeaux, a youth comely enough. O Alinda, too comely, else hadst not thou been thus discontent; valiant, and that fettered thine eye; wise, else hadst not thou not been now won; but for all these virtues banished by thy father, and therefore if he know thy parentage he will hate the fruit for the tree, and condemn the young scion for the old stock. Well, howsoever, I must love, and whomsoever, I will, and, whatsoever betide, Aliena will think well of Saladyn, suppose he of me as he please.' And with that fetching a deep sigh, she rose up and went to Ganymede, who all this while sat in a great dump, fearing the imminent danger of her friend Rosader; but now Aliena began to comfort her, herself being overgrown with sorrows, and to recall her from her melancholy with many pleasant persuasions. Ganymede took all in the best part, and so they went home together after they had folded their flocks, supping with old Corydon, who had provided their cates. He, after supper, to pass away the night while bedtime, began a long discourse, how Montanus, the young shepherd that was in love with Phoebe, could by no means obtain any favour at her hands, but still pained in restless passions remained a hopeless and perplexed lover. 'I would I might,' quoth Aliena, 'once see that Phoebe. Is she so fair that she thinks no shepherd worthy of her beauty, or so froward that no love nor loyalty will content her, or so coy that she requires a long time to be wooed, or so foolish that she forgets that like a fop she must have a large harvest for a little corn?'

'I cannot distinguish,' quoth Corydon, 'of these nice qualities, but one of these days I'll bring Montanus and her down, that you may both see their persons and note their passions, and then where the blame is, there let it rest. But this I am sure,' quoth Corydon, 'if all maidens were of her mind the world would grow to a mad pass, for there would be great store of wooing and little wedding, many words and little worship, much folly and no faith.' At this sad sentence of Corydon, so solemnly brought forth, Aliena smiled, and because it waxed late, she and her page went to bed, both of them having fleas in their ears to keep them awake, Ganymede for the hurt of her Rosader, and Aliena for the affection she bore to Saladyn. In this discontented humour they passed away the time, till falling on sleep, their senses at rest, love left them to their quiet slumbers, which were not long, for as soon as Phoebus rose from his Aurora and began to mount him in the sky, summoning the plough-swains to their handy labour, Aliena arose, and going to the couch where Ganymede lay, awakened her page and said the morning was far spent, the dew small, and time called them away to their folds. 'Ah, ah,' quoth Ganymede, 'is the wind in that door? Then in faith I perceive that there is no diamond so hard but will yield to the file, no cedar so strong but the wind will shake, nor any mind so chaste but love will change. Well Aliena, must Saladyn be the man, and will it be a match? Trust me, he is fair and valiant, the son of a worthy knight, whom if he imitate in perfection as he represents him in proportion, he is worthy of no less than Aliena. But he is an exile. What then? I hope my mistress respects the virtues not the wealth, and measures the qualities not the substance. Those dames that are like Danae, that like Jove in no shape but in a shower of gold, I wish them husbands with much wealth and little wit, that the want of the one may blemish the abundance of the other. It should, my Aliena, stain the honour of a shepherd's life to set the end of passions upon pelf. Love's eyes looks not so low as gold, there is no fees to be paid in Cupid's courts, and in elder time, as Corydon hath told me, the shepherd's love-gifts were apples and chestnuts, and then their desires were loyal and their thoughts constant. But now

Quaerenda pecunia primum, post nummos virtus.[1]

And the time is grown to that which Horace in his Satires wrote on:
omnis enim res
Virtus fama decus divina humanaque pulchris
Divitiis parent: quas qui constrinxerit ille
Clarus erit, fortis, iustus, sapiens, etiam et rex
Et quicquid volet—[2]

But Aliena, let it not be so with thee in thy fancies, but respect his faith, and there an end.' Aliena, hearing Ganymede thus forward to further Saladyn in his affections, thought she kissed the child for the nurse's sake, and wooed for him that she might please Rosader, made this reply: 'Why Ganymede, whereof grows this persuasion? Hast thou seen love in my

---

1. *Quaerenda ... virtus*] Latin: Seek money first, virtue after cash. See p. 43 n. 1.
2. *omnis ... volet*] Latin: For virtue, fame, honour, all things divine and human submit to beautiful riches. Whoever secures wealth will be distinguished, strong, just, wise, even a king, and whatever else he wishes (Horace, *Satires*, 2.3.94).

looks? Or are mine eyes grown so amorous that they discover some new-entertained fancies? If thou measurest my thoughts by my countenance, thou mayst prove as ill a physiognomer as the lapidary that aims at the secret virtues of the topaz by the exterior shadow of the stone. The operation of the agate is not known by the streaks, nor the diamond prized by his brightness, but by his hardness. The carbuncle that shineth most is not ever the most precious, and the apothecaries choose not flowers for their colours, but for their virtues. Women's faces are not always calendars of fancy, nor do their thoughts and their looks ever agree, for when their eyes are fullest of favours, then they are oft most empty of desire, and when they seem to frown at disdain, then are they most forward to affection. If I be melancholy, then, Ganymede, 'tis not a consequence that I am entangled with the perfection of Saladyn. But seeing fire cannot be hid in the straw, nor love kept so covert but it will be spied, what should friends conceal fancies? Know, my Ganymede, the beauty and valour, the wit and prowess of Saladyn hath fettered Aliena so far as there is no object pleasing to her eyes but the sight of Saladyn, and if Love have done me justice to wrap his thoughts in the folds of my face,[1] and that he be as deeply enamoured as I am passionate, I tell thee Ganymede, there shall not be much wooing, for she is already won, and what needs a longer battery.' 'I am glad,' quoth Ganymede, 'that it shall be thus proportioned, you to match with Saladyn, and I with Rosader; thus have the Destinies favoured us with some pleasing aspect, that have made us as private in our loves as familiar in our fortunes.'

With this Ganymede start up, made her ready, and went into the fields with Aliena. Where, unfolding their flocks, they sat them down under an olive tree, both of them amorous, and yet diversely affected; Aliena joying in the excellence of Saladyn, and Ganymede sorrowing for the wounds of her Rosader, not quiet in thought till she might hear of his health. As thus both of them sat in their dumps, they might espy where Corydon came running towards them, almost out of breath with his haste. 'What news with you,' quoth Aliena, 'that you come in such post?' 'O mistress,' quoth Corydon, 'you have a long time desired to see Phoebe, the fair shepherdess whom Montanus loves. So now if it please you and Ganymede but to walk with me to yonder thicket, there shall you see Montanus and her sitting by a fountain, he courting with his country ditties, and she as coy as if she held love in disdain.'

The news were so welcome to the two lovers that up they rose and went with Corydon. As soon as they drew nigh the thicket, they might espy where Phoebe sat, the fairest shepherdess in all Arden, and he the frolickest

---

1. face] Q2 (Q1 reads 'fare').

swain in the whole forest, she in a petticoat of scarlet covered with a green mantle, and to shroud her from the sun a chaplet[1] of roses, from under which appeared a face full of Nature's excellence, and two such eyes as might have amated[2] a greater man than Montanus. At gaze upon this gorgeous nymph sat the shepherd, feeding his eyes with her favours, wooing with such piteous looks, and courting with such deep-strained sighs as would have made Diana herself to have been compassionate. At last, fixing his looks on the riches of her face, his head on his hand and his elbow on his knee, he sung this mournful ditty:

Montanus' Sonnet.

> A turtle sat upon a leafless tree,
> Mourning her absent fere[3]
> With sad and sorry cheer:
> About her wondering stood
> The citizens of wood,
> And whilst her plumes she rents
> And for her love laments,
> The stately trees complain them,
> The birds with sorrow pain them;
> Each one that doth her view
> Her pain and sorrows rue.
> But were the sorrows known
> That me hath overthrown,
> Oh how would Phoebe sigh if she did look on me!
>
> The lovesick Polypheme[4] that could not see,
> Who on the barren shore
> His fortunes doth deplore,
> And melteth all in moan
> For Galatea[5] gone,
> And with his piteous cries
> Afflicts both earth and skies,

---

1. chaplet] Wreath for the head, usually a garland of flowers or leaves.
2. amated] Overwhelmed, confounded.
3. fere] Companion, mate.
4. Polypheme] Greek myth; Polyphemus, the Cyclops or one-eyed giant in Homer's *Odyssey*. His one eye is destroyed by Odysseus in attempting to escape from Polyphemus' cave.
5. Galatea] Greek sea-nymph wooed by the ugly Cyclops.

And to his woe betook
Doth break both pipe and hook,
For whom complains the morn,
For whom the sea-nymphs mourn,
Alas, his pain is nought,
For were my woe but thought,
Oh how would Phoebe sigh if she did look on me!

Beyond compare my pain,
    Yet glad am I,
If gentle Phoebe deign
    To see her Montan die.

After this, Montanus felt his passions so extreme that he fell into this exclamation against the injustice of Love:

Hélas, tyran, plein de rigueur,
Modère un peu ta violence:
Que te sert si grande dépense?
C'est trop de flammes pour un coeur.
Épargnez en une étincelle,
Puis fais ton effort d'émouvoir,
La fière qui ne veut point voir,
En quel feu je brûle pour elle.
Exécute, Amour, ce dessein,
Et rabaisse un peu son audace:
Son coeur ne doit être de glace,
Bien qu'elle ait de neige le sein.[1]

Montanus ended his sonnet with such a volley of sighs and such a stream of tears as might have moved any but Phoebe to have granted him favour. But she, measuring all his passions with a coy disdain, and triumphing in the poor shepherd's pathetical humours, smiling at his martyrdom as though love had been no malady, scornfully warbled out this sonnet:

---

1. Hélas … sein] French: Alas, harsh tyrant, restrain your force a little: what good is such a great expense of it? Here are too many flames for one heart. Spare a spark of them, then try to move the proud girl who does not wish to see in what fire I burn for her. Do this, Love, and lessen her presumption a little; her heart should not be of ice, although she has a breast of snow.

Phoebe's Sonnet: a Reply to Montanus' Passion.

Down a down,
 Thus Phyllis sung
 By fancy once distressed:
Whoso by foolish Love are stung
 Are worthily oppressed.
 And so sing I. With a down, down, etc.

When Love was first begot,
And by the mover's will
Did fall to human lot
His solace to fulfil,
Devoid of all deceit,
A chaste and holy fire
Did quicken man's conceit,
And women's breast inspire.
The gods that saw the good
That mortals did approve,
With kind and holy mood
Began to talk of Love.
 Down a down.
 Thus Phyllis sung
 By fancy once distressed, etc.
But during this accord,
A wonder strange to hear:
Whilst Love in deed and word
Most faithful did appear,
False-semblance came in place,
By jealousy attended,
And with a double face
Both love and fancy blended;
Which made the gods forsake,
And men from fancy fly,
And maidens scorn a make,[1]
Forsooth, and so will I.
 Down a down.
 Thus Phyllis sung
 By fancy once distressed;

---

1. make] Mate or spouse.

> Who so by foolish Love are stung
> Are worthily oppressed.
> And so sing I.
> With down a down, a down down, a down a.

Montanus, hearing the cruel resolution of Phoebe, was so overgrown with passions that from amorous ditties he fell flat into these terms: 'Ah Phoebe,' quoth he, 'whereof art thou made that thou regardest not my malady? Am I so hateful an object that thine eyes condemn me for an abject, or so base that thy desires cannot stoop so low as to lend me a gracious look? My passions are many, my loves more, my thoughts loyalty, and my fancy faith, all devoted in humble devoir [1] to the service of Phoebe. And shall I reap no reward for such fealties? The swain's daily labours is quit with the evening's hire, the ploughman's toil is eased with the hope of corn, what the ox sweats out at the plough he fatteneth at the crib, but unfortunate Montanus hath no salve for his sorrows, nor any hope of recompense for the hazard of his perplexed passions. If, Phoebe, time may plead the proof of my truth, twice seven winters have I loved fair Phoebe. If constancy be a cause to farther my suit, Montanus' thoughts have been sealed in the sweet of Phoebe's excellence, as far from change as she from love. If outward passions may discover inward affections, the furrows in my face may decipher the sorrows of my heart, and the map of my looks the griefs of my mind. Thou seest, Phoebe, the tears of despair have made my cheeks full of wrinkles and my scalding sighs have made the air echo her pity conceived in my plaints. Philomel hearing my passions hath left her mournful tunes to listen to the discourse of my miseries. I have portrayed in every tree the beauty of my mistress and the despair of my loves. What is it in the woods cannot witness my woes, and who is it would not pity my plaints? Only Phoebe. And why? Because I am Montanus, and she Phoebe, I a worthless swain, and she the most excellent of all fairs. Beautiful Phoebe, oh, might I say pitiful, then happy were I though I tasted but one minute of that good hap! Measure Montanus not by his fortunes but by his loves, and balance not his wealth but his desires, and lend but one gracious look to cure a heap of disquieted cares. If not, ah, if Phoebe cannot love, let a storm of frowns end the discontent of my thoughts, and so let me perish in my desires because they are above my deserts. Only at my death this favour cannot be denied me, that all shall say Montanus died for love of hard-hearted Phoebe.' At these words she filled her face full of frowns and made him this short and sharp reply:

---

1. devoir] Duty (from French).

'Importunate shepherd, whose loves are lawless, because restless. Are thy passions so extreme that thou canst not conceal them with patience, or art thou so folly-sick that thou must needs be fancy-sick, and in thy affections tied to such an exigent as none serves but Phoebe? Well sir, if your market may be made nowhere else, home again: for your mart is at the fairest. Phoebe is no lettuce for your lips, and her grapes hangs so high that gaze at them you may, but touch them you cannot. Yet, Montanus, I speak not this in pride, but in disdain; not that I scorn thee, but that I hate love, for I count it as great honour to triumph over fancy as over fortune. Rest thee content therefore Montanus, cease from thy loves, and bridle thy looks, quench the sparkles before they grow to a further flame, for in loving me thou shalt live by loss, and what thou utterest in words are all written in the wind. Wert thou, Montanus, as fair as Paris, as hardy as Hector,[1] as constant as Troilus,[2] as loving as Leander,[3] Phoebe could not love because she cannot love at all, and therefore if thou pursue me with Phoebus I must fly with Daphne.'[4]

Ganymede, overhearing all these passions of Montanus, could not brook the cruelty of Phoebe, but starting from behind the bush said: 'And if, damsel, you fled from me I would transform you as Daphne to a bay, and then in contempt trample your branches under my feet.' Phoebe at this sudden reply was amazed, especially when she saw so fair a swain as Ganymede. Blushing therefore, she would have been gone but that he held her by the hand and prosecuted his reply thus: 'What shepherdess, so fair and so cruel? Disdain beseems not cottages, nor coyness maids, for either they be condemned to be too proud or too froward. Take heed, fair nymph, that in despising love you be not overreached with love, and in shaking off all, shape yourself to your own shadow, and so with Narcissus prove passionate and yet unpitied. Oft have I heard, and sometimes have I seen, high disdain turned to hot desires. Because thou art beautiful, be not so coy; as there is nothing more fair, so there is nothing more fading; as momentary as the shadows which grows from a cloudy sun. Such, my

---

1.   Hector] Greek legend; eldest son of Priam, King of Troy; leader and bravest of the Trojans during the siege of Troy.
2.   Troilus] Greek myth; a younger son of Priam. 'Constant' refers to the post-classical story of Troilus and Cressida as told by Chaucer and later Shakespeare.
3.   Leander] Youth of Abydus who, according to legend, was in love with Hero, the beautiful priestess of Aphrodite at Sestus on the opposite shore. Leander would swim across each night guided by a tower light, but one stormy night the light was extinguished and Leander drowned.
4.   Daphne] Greek myth; a nymph who was saved from the amorous attentions of Apollo by being changed into a laurel tree.

fair shepherdess, as disdain in youth, desire in age, and then are they hated in the winter, that might have been loved in the prime. A wrinkled maid is like to a parched rose that is cast up in coffers to please the smell, not worn in the hand to content the eye. There is no folly in love to *had I wist*, and therefore be ruled by me: love while thou art young, lest thou be disdained when thou art old. Beauty nor time cannot be recalled, and if thou love, like of Montanus, for as his desires are many, so his deserts are great.'

Phoebe all this while gazed on the perfection of Ganymede, as deeply enamoured on his perfection as Montanus inveigled with hers, for her eye made survey of his excellent feature, which she found so rare that she thought the ghost of Adonis[1] had been leapt from Elysium[2] in the shape of a swain.[3] When she blushed at her own folly to look so long on a stranger, she mildly made answer to Ganymede thus: 'I cannot deny, sir, but I have heard of Love, though I never felt love, and have read of such a goddess as Venus, though I never saw any but her picture, and perhaps—' and with that she waxed red and bashful, and withal silent, which Ganymede perceiving, commended in herself the bashfulness of the maid and desired her to go forward. 'And perhaps, sir,' quoth she, 'mine eye hath been more prodigal today than ever before—' and with that she stayed again, as one greatly passionate and perplexed. Aliena, seeing the hare through the maze, bade her forward with her prattle, but in vain, for at this abrupt period she broke off, and with her eyes full of tears, and her face covered with a vermilion dye, she sat down and sighed. Whereupon Aliena and Ganymede, seeing the shepherdess in such a strange plight, left Phoebe with her Montanus, wishing her friendly that she would be more pliant to love, lest in penance Venus joined her to some sharp repentance. Phoebe made no reply, but fetched such a sigh that Echo[4] made relation of her plaint, giving Ganymede such an adieu with a piercing glance that the amorous girl-boy perceived Phoebe was pinched by the heel.[5]

But leaving Phoebe to the follies of her new fancy, and Montanus to attend upon her – to Saladyn, who all this last night could not rest for the remembrance of Aliena, insomuch that he framed a sweet conceited sonnet to content his humour, which he put in his bosom, being requested

---

1. Adonis] Greek myth; a handsome youth loved by Aphrodite. Killed by a wild boar, he was believed to spend part of the year in the underworld and part on earth.
2. Elysium] The dwelling-place of the blessed after death.
3. swain] A country youth.
4. Echo] Nymph deprived of speech by the goddess Hera except for repeating the last words of her interlocutor. After falling in love with Narcissus and being rejected by him, she wasted away to a voice.
5. pinched by the heel] Caught.

by his brother Rosader to go to Aliena and Ganymede to signify unto them that his wounds were not dangerous. A more happy message could not happen to Saladyn, that taking his forest bill on his neck, he trudgeth in all haste towards the plains where Aliena's flocks did feed, coming just to the place when they returned from Montanus and Phoebe. Fortune so conducted this jolly forester that he encountered them and Corydon, whom he presently saluted in this manner:

'Fair shepherdess – and too fair, unless your beauty be tempered with courtesy and the lineaments of the face graced with the lowliness of mind – as many good fortunes to you and your page as yourselves can desire or I imagine. My brother Rosader, in the grief of his green wounds still mindful of his friends, hath sent me to you with a kind salute, to show that he brooks his pains with the more patience, in that he holds the parties precious in whose defence he received the prejudice. The report of your welfare will be a great comfort to his distempered body and distressed thoughts, and therefore he sent me with a strict charge to visit you.' 'And you,' quoth Aliena, 'are the more welcome in that you are messenger from so kind a gentleman, whose pains we compassionate with as great sorrow as he brooks them with grief, and his wounds breeds in us as many passions as in him extremities, so that what disquiet he feels in body we partake in heart, wishing, if we might, that our mishap might salve his malady. But seeing our wills yields him little ease, our orisons are never idle to the gods for his recovery.' 'I pray, youth,' quoth Ganymede with tears in his eyes, 'when the surgeon searched him, held he his wounds dangerous?' 'Dangerous,' quoth Saladyn, 'but not mortal, and the sooner to be cured in that his patient is not impatient of any pains, whereupon my brother hopes within these ten days to walk abroad and visit you himself.' 'In the meantime,' quoth Ganymede, 'say his Rosalynd commends her to him and bids him be of good cheer.' 'I know not,' quoth Saladyn, 'who that Rosalynd is, but whatsoever she is, her name is never out of his mouth, but amidst the deepest of his passions he useth Rosalynd as a charm to appease all sorrows with patience. Insomuch that I conjecture my brother is in love, and she some paragon that holds his heart perplexed, whose name he oft records with sighs, sometimes with tears, straight with joy, then with smiles, as if in one person love had lodged a chaos of confused passions. Wherein I have noted the variable disposition of fancy, that like the polyp in colours, so it changeth into sundry humours, being as it should seem a combat mixed with disquiet and a bitter pleasure wrapped in a sweet prejudice, like to the sinople[1] tree whose blossoms delight the smell and whose fruit infects the taste.' 'By my faith,' quoth Aliena, 'sir,

---

1.   sinople] Green, a heraldic term.

you are deep read in love, or grows your insight into affection by experience? Howsoever, you are a great philosopher in Venus' principles, else could you not discover her secret aphorisms. But, sir, our country amours are not like your courtly fancies, nor is our wooing like your suing, for poor shepherds never plain them till love pain them, where the courtier's eyes is full of passions when his heart is most free from affection. They court to discover their eloquence, we woo to ease our sorrows. Every fair face with them must have a new fancy sealed with a forefinger kiss and a far-fetched sigh, we here love one, and live to that one so long as life can maintain love, using few ceremonies because we know few subtleties, and little eloquence for that we lightly account of flattery; only faith and troth, that's shepherds' wooing; and, sir, how like you of this?' 'So,' quoth Saladyn, 'as I could tie myself to such love.' 'What, and look so low as a shepherdess, being the son of Sir John of Bordeaux? Such desires were a disgrace to your honours.' And with that, surveying exquisitely every part of him, as uttering all these words in a deep passion, she espied the paper in his bosom, whereupon growing jealous that it was some amorous sonnet, she suddenly snatched it out of his bosom and asked if it were any secret. She was bashful and Saladyn blushed, which she perceiving said: 'Nay then, sir, if you wax red, my life for yours 'tis some love-matter. I will see your mistress' name, her praises, and your passions.' And with that she looked on it, which was written to this effect:

Saladyn's Sonnet.

If it be true that heaven's eternal course
With restless sway and ceaseless turning glides,
If air inconstant be and swelling source
Turn and returns with many fluent tides,
    If earth in winter summer's pride estrange,
    And Nature seemeth only fair in change;

If it be true that our immortal spright
Derived from heavenly pure, in wandering still,
In novelty and strangeness doth delight,
And by discoverent power discerneth ill;
    And if the body for to work his best
    Doth with the seasons change his place of rest;

Whence comes it that, enforced by furious skies,
I change both place and soil, but not my heart,
Yet salve not in this change my maladies?
Whence grows it that each object works my smart?

Alas I see my faith procures my miss,
And change in love against my nature is.

Et florida pungunt.[1]

Aliena having read over his sonnet began thus pleasantly to descant upon it. 'I see, Saladyn,' quoth she, 'that as the sun is no sun without his brightness, nor the diamond accounted for precious unless it be hard, so men are not men unless they be in love, and their honours are measured by their amours not their labours, counting it more commendable for a gentleman to be full of fancy than full of virtue. I had thought,

Otia si tollas, periere Cupidinis arcus,
Contemptaeque iacent et sine luce faces.[2]

But I see Ovid's axiom is not authentical, for even labour hath her loves, and extremity is no pumice-stone to rase out fancy. Yourself exiled from your wealth, friends, and country by Torismond, sorrows enough to suppress affections, yet amidst the depth of these extremities love will be lord, and show his power to be more predominant than Fortune. But I pray you, sir, if without offence I may crave it, are they some new thoughts, or some old desires?' Saladyn, that now saw opportunity pleasant, thought to strike while the iron was hot, and therefore, taking Aliena by the hand, sat down by her; and Ganymede, to give them leave to their loves, found herself busy about the folds, whilst Saladyn fell into this prattle with Aliena:

'Fair mistress, if I be blunt in discovering my affections, and use little eloquence in levelling out my loves, I appeal for pardon to your own principles that say shepherds use few ceremonies, for that they acquaint themselves with few subtleties. To frame myself, therefore, to your country fashion with much faith and little flattery, know, beautiful shepherdess, that whilst I lived in the court I knew not love's cumber,[3] but I held affection as a toy, not as a malady, using fancy as the Hyperborei do their flowers, which they wear in their bosom all day and cast them in the fire for fuel at night. I liked all because I loved none, and who was most fair, on her I fed mine eye, but as charily as the bee, that as soon as she hath sucked honey from the rose, flies straight to the next marigold. Living thus at mine own list, I wondered at such as were in love, and when I read their passions I took them only for poems that flowed from the quickness

---

1. *Et florida pungunt*] Latin: Even flowers sting.
2. *Otia … faces*] Latin: Take away leisure and Cupid's bow is broken, and his torch lies extinguished and despised (Ovid, *Remedia Amoris*, 139).
3. cumber] Encumbrance.

of the wit, not the sorrows of the heart. But now, fair nymph, since I became a forester, Love hath taught me such a lesson that I must confess his deity and dignity, and say as there is nothing so precious as beauty, so there is nothing more piercing than fancy. For since first I arrived in this place, and mine eye took a curious survey of your excellence, I have been so fettered with your beauty and virtue as, sweet Aliena, Saladyn without further circumstance loves Aliena. I could paint out my desires with long ambages, but seeing in many words lies mistrust, and that truth is ever naked, let this suffice for a country wooing: Saladyn loves Aliena, and none but Aliena.'

Although these words were most heavenly harmony in the ears of the shepherdess, yet to seem coy at the first courting, and to disdain love howsoever she desired love, she made this reply:

'Ah Saladyn, though I seem simple, yet I am more subtle than to swallow the hook because it hath a painted bait. As men are wily so women are wary, especially if they have that wit by others' harms to beware. Do we not know, Saladyn, that men's tongues are like Mercury's[1] pipe, that can enchant Argus[2] with an hundred eyes, and their words as prejudicial as the charms of Circe[3] that transform men into monsters. If such Sirens sing, we poor women had need stop our ears, lest in hearing we prove so foolish-hardy as to believe them, and so perish in trusting much and suspecting little. Saladyn, *Piscator ictus sapit*,[4] he that hath been once poisoned, and afterwards fears not to bowse of every potion, is worthy to suffer double penance. Give me leave then to mistrust, though I do not condemn. Saladyn is now in love with Aliena, he a gentleman of great parentage, she a shepherdess of mean parents, he honourable and she poor? Can love consist of contraries? Will the falcon perch with the kestrel,[5] the lion harbour with the wolf? Will Venus join robes and rags together, or can there be a sympathy between a king and a beggar? Then Saladyn, how can I believe thee that love should unite our thoughts when Fortune hath set such a difference between our degrees? But suppose thou likest of Aliena's beauty: men in their fancy resemble the wasp, which scorns that flower from which she hath fetched her wax; playing like the inhabitants

---

1. Mercury] In Roman religion, the messenger of the gods; identified with the Greek god Hermes and, like him, the god of eloquent speech.
2. Argus] A giant with a hundred eyes. After he was killed by Hermes, his eyes were transferred to the peacock's tale.
3. Circe] In Homer's *Odyssey* (Bk 10), a goddess living on the fabulous island of Aeaea, powerful in magic, who turned Odysseus' men into swine.
4. *Piscator ictus sapit*] Latin: The fisher stricken will be wise.
5. kestrel] Misprinted in Q1 as 'Kistresse'.

of the island Tenerife, who when they have gathered the sweet spices, use the trees for fuel. So men, when they have glutted themselves with the fair of women's faces, hold them for necessary evils, and wearied with that which they seemed so much to love, cast away fancy as children do their rattles, and loathing that which so deeply before they liked, especially such as take love in a minute and have their eyes attractive like jet apt to entertain any object, are as ready to let it slip again. Saladyn, hearing how Aliena harped still upon one string, which was the doubt of men's constancy, he broke off her sharp invective thus:

'I grant, Aliena,' quoth he, 'many men have done amiss in proving soon ripe and soon rotten, but particular instances infer no general conclusions, and therefore I hope what others have faulted in shall not prejudice my favours. I will not use sophistry to confirm my love, for that is subtlety, nor long discourses, lest my words might be thought more than my faith, but if this will suffice: that by the honour of a gentleman I love Aliena, and woo Aliena not to crop the blossoms and reject the tree, but to consummate my faithful desires in the honourable end of marriage.'

At this word marriage, Aliena stood in a maze what to answer, fearing that if she were too coy, to drive him away with her disdain, and if she were too courteous, to discover the heat of her desires. In a dilemma thus what to do, at last this she said: 'Saladyn, ever since I saw thee, I favoured thee. I cannot dissemble my desires, because I see thou dost faithfully manifest thy thoughts, and in liking thee I love thee so far as mine honour holds fancy still in suspense, but if I knew thee as virtuous as thy father, or as well qualified as thy brother Rosader, the doubt should be quickly decided. But for this time, to give thee an answer, assure thyself this: I will either marry with Saladyn or still live a virgin.' And with this they strained one another's hand. Which Ganymede espying, thinking he had had his mistress long enough at shrift, said: 'What, a match or no?' 'A match,' quoth Aliena, 'or else it were an ill market.' 'I am glad,' quoth Ganymede, 'I would Rosader were well here to make up a mess.'[1] 'Well remembered,' quoth Saladyn, 'I forgot I left my brother Rosader alone, and therefore lest being solitary he should increase his sorrows, I will haste me to him. May it please you then to command me any service to him, I am ready to be a dutiful messenger.' 'Only at this time commend me to him,' quoth Aliena, 'and tell him, though we cannot pleasure him, we pray for him.' 'And forget not,' quoth Ganymede, 'my commendations, but say to him that Rosalynd sheds as many tears from her heart as he drops of blood from his wounds, for the sorrow of his misfortunes, feathering all her thoughts with disquiet till his welfare procure her content. Say thus, good

---

1. mess] Company, group collected together (usually to eat).

Saladyn, and so farewell.' He having his message, gave a courteous adieu to them both, especially to Aliena, and so playing loath to depart, went to his brother. But Aliena, she perplexed and yet joyful, passed away the day pleasantly, still praising the perfection of Saladyn, not ceasing to chat of her new love till evening drew on, and then they, folding their sheep, went home to bed. Where we leave them and return to Phoebe.

Phoebe, fired with the uncouth flame of love, returned to her father's house so galled with restless passions as now she began to acknowledge that as there was no flower so fresh but might be parched with the sun, no tree so strong but might be shaken with a storm, so there was no thought so chaste but Time, armed with Love, could make amorous, for she that held Diana for the goddess of her devotion was now fain to fly to the altar of Venus, as suppliant now with prayers as she was froward afore with disdain. As she lay in her bed, she called to mind the several beauties of young Ganymede; first his locks, which being amber-hued, passeth the wreath that Phoebus puts on to make his front glorious; his brow of ivory was like the seat where love and majesty sits enthroned to enchain fancy; his eyes as bright as the burnishing of the heaven, darting forth frowns with disdain and smiles with favour, lightning such looks as would inflame desire were she wrapped in the circle of the frozen zone;[1] in his cheeks the vermilion teinture of the rose flourished upon natural alabaster, the blush of the morn and Luna's silver show were so lively portrayed that the Trojan[2] that fills out wine to Jupiter was not half so beautiful; his face was full of pleasance, and all the rest of his lineaments proportioned with such excellence as Phoebe was fettered in the sweetness of his feature. The idea of these perfections tumbling in her mind made the poor shepherdess so perplexed, as feeling a pleasure tempered with intolerable pains, and yet a disquiet mixed with a content, she rather wished to die than to live in this amorous anguish. But wishing is little worth in such extremes, and therefore was she forced to pine in her malady without any salve for her sorrows. Reveal it she durst not, as daring in such matters to make none her secretary; and to conceal it, why, it doubled her grief, for as fire suppressed grows to the greater flame, and the current stopped to the more violent stream, so love smothered wrings the heart with the deeper passions.

Perplexed thus with sundry agonies, her food began to fail and the disquiet of her mind began to work a distemperature of her body, that, to be short, Phoebe fell extreme sick, and so sick as there was almost left no recovery of health. Her father, seeing his fair Phoebe thus distressed,

---

1. circle of the frozen zone] The Arctic.
2. Trojan] The original Ganymede, abducted by Jupiter and made his cup-bearer.

sent for his friends, who sought by medicine to cure and by counsel to pacify, but all in vain, for although her body was feeble through long fasting, yet she did *magis aegrotare animo quam corpore.*[1] Which her friends perceived and sorrowed at, but salve it they could not.

The news of her sickness was bruited abroad through all the forest, which no sooner came to Montanus' ear, but he like a madman came to visit Phoebe. Where sitting by her bedside, he began his exordium with so many tears and sighs, that she, perceiving the extremity of his sorrows, began now as a lover to pity them, although Ganymede held her from redressing them. Montanus craved to know the cause of her sickness, tempered with secret plaints, but she answered him, as the rest, with silence, having still the form of Ganymede in her mind, and conjecturing how she might reveal her loves. To utter it in words she found herself too bashful, to discourse by any friend she would not trust any in her amours, to remain thus perplexed still and conceal all, it was a double death. Whereupon for her last refuge she resolved to write unto Ganymede, and therefore desired Montanus to absent himself awhile but not to depart, for she would see if she could steal a nap. He was no sooner gone out of the chamber, but reaching to her standish,[2] she took pen and paper and wrote a letter to this effect:

Phoebe to Ganymede wisheth what she wants herself.

Fair shepherd – and therefore is Phoebe unfortunate because thou art so fair – although hitherto mine eyes were adamants to resist love, yet I no sooner saw thy face but they became amorous to entertain love, more devoted to fancy than before they were repugnant to affection, addicted to the one by nature, and drawn to the other by beauty, which, being rare and made the more excellent by many virtues, hath so snared the freedom of Phoebe as she rests at thy mercy, either to be made the most fortunate of all maidens, or the most miserable of all women. Measure not, Ganymede, my loves by my wealth, nor my desires by my degrees, but think my thoughts are as full of faith as thy face of amiable favours. Then, as thou knowest thyself most beautiful, suppose me most constant. If thou deemest me hard-hearted because I hated Montanus, think I was forced to it by fate. If thou sayst I am kind-hearted because so lightly I love thee at the first look, think I was driven to it by destiny, whose influence, as it is mighty, so it is not to be resisted. If my fortunes were anything but infortunate love, I would strive with fortune, but he that wrests against the will of

---

1. *magis ... corpore*] Latin: more sickened in mind than in body.
2. standish] Ink-stand.

Venus seeks to quench fire with oil, and to thrust out one thorn by putting in another. If then, Ganymede, love enters at the eye, harbours in the heart, and will neither be driven out with physic nor reason, pity me as one whose malady hath no salve but from thy sweet self, whose grief hath no ease but through thy grant, and think I am a virgin who is deeply wronged when I am forced to woo, and conjecture love to be strong that is more forcible than nature.

Thus distressed, unless by thee eased, I expect either to live fortunate by thy favour or die miserable by thy denial. Living in hope. Farewell.

She that must be thine, or
not be at all.
Phoebe.

To this letter she annexed this sonnet:

Sonnetto.

My boat doth pass the straights
    of seas incensed with fire,
Filled with forgetfulness;
    amidst the winter's night,
A blind and careless boy,
    brought up by fond desire,
Doth guide me in the sea
    of sorrow and despite.

For every oar, he sets
    a rank of foolish thoughts,
And cuts, instead of wave,
    a hope without distress;
The winds of my deep sighs,
    that thunder still for noughts,
Have split my sails with fear,
    with care, with heaviness.

A mighty storm of tears,
    a black and hideous cloud,
A thousand fierce disdains
    do slack the halyards[1] oft;
Till ignorance do pull
    and error hail the shrouds,

---

lyards] A rope or tackle used for raising or lowering a sail, yard, spar or flag.

No star for safety shines,
           no Phoebe from aloft.

Time hath subdued art,
           and joy is slave to woe:
Alas, Love's guide, be kind;
           what, shall I perish so?

This letter and the sonnet being ended, she could find no fit messenger
to send it by, and therefore she called in Montanus, and entreated him to
carry it to Ganymede. Although poor Montanus saw day at a little hole,
and did perceive what passion pinched her, yet, that he might seem dutiful
to his mistress in all service, he dissembled the matter and became a willing messenger of his own martyrdom. And so, taking the letter, went the
next morn very early to the plains where Aliena fed her flocks, and there
he found Ganymede sitting under a pomegranate tree sorrowing for the
hard fortunes of her Rosader. Montanus saluted him, and according to his
charge delivered Ganymede the letters, which, he said, came from Phoebe.
At this the wanton blushed, as being abashed to think what news should
come from an unknown shepherdess, but taking the letters, unripped the
seals and read over the discourse of Phoebe's fancies. When she had read
and over-read them Ganymede began to smile, and looking on Montanus
fell into a great laughter, and with that called Aliena, to whom she showed
the writings. Who, having perused them, conceited them very pleasantly
and smiled to see how love had yoked her who before disdained to stoop
to the lure.[1] Aliena whispering Ganymede in the ear, and saying, 'Knew
Phoebe what want there were in thee to perform her will, and how unfit
thy kind is to be kind to her, she would be more wise and less enamoured;
but leaving that, I pray thee let us sport with this swain.' At that word,
Ganymede, turning to Montanus, began to glance at him thus:

'I pray thee tell me, shepherd, by those sweet thoughts and pleasing
sighs that grow from my mistress' favours, art thou in love with Phoebe?'
'O my youth,' quoth Montanus, 'were Phoebe so far in love with me, my
flocks would be more fat and their master more quiet, for through the
sorrows of my discontent grows the leanness of my sheep.' 'Alas poor
swain,' quoth Ganymede, 'are thy passions so extreme, or thy fancy so
resolute, that no reason will blemish the pride of thy affection and rase out
that which thou strivest for without hope?' 'Nothing can make me forget
Phoebe, while Montanus forget himself, for those characters which true
love hath stamped neither the envy of Time nor Fortune can wipe away.'

---

1. lure] An apparatus used by falconers to recall their hawks. Used in the
   phrase 'to stoop to the lure'; under command, control.

'Why but Montanus,' quoth Ganymede, 'enter with a deep insight into the despair of thy fancies and thou shalt see the depth of thine own follies, for, poor man, thy progress in love is a regress to loss, swimming against the stream with the crab, and flying with Apis Indica[1] against wind and weather. Thou seekest with Phoebus to win Daphne, and she flies faster than thou canst follow; thy desires soar with the hobby, but her disdain reacheth higher than thou canst make wing. I tell thee Montanus, in courting Phoebe thou barkest with the wolves of Syria against the moon, and rovest at such a mark with thy thoughts as is beyond the pitch of thy bow, praying to Love when Love is pitiless and thy malady remediless. For proof, Montanus, read these letters, wherein thou shalt see thy great follies and little hope.'

With that Montanus took them and perused them, but with such sorrow in his looks as they bewrayed a source of confused passions in his heart. At every line his colour changed, and every sentence was ended with a period of sighs.

At last, noting Phoebe's extreme desire toward Ganymede and her disdain towards him, giving Ganymede the letter, the shepherd stood as though he had neither won nor lost. Which Ganymede perceiving, wakened him out his dream thus: 'Now Montanus, dost thou see thou vowest great service and obtainest but little reward, but in lieu of thy loyalty she maketh thee as Bellerophon[2] carry thine own bane. Then drink not willingly of that potion wherein thou knowest is poison, creep not to her that cares not for thee. What, Montanus, there are many as fair as Phoebe, but most of all more courteous than Phoebe. I tell thee shepherd, favour is love's fuel, then since thou canst not get that, let the flame vanish into smoke, and rather sorrow for a while than repent thee for ever.'

'I tell thee, Ganymede,' quoth Montanus, 'as they which are stung with the scorpion cannot be recovered but by the scorpion, nor he that was wounded with Achilles' lance be cured but with the same truncheon, so Apollo was fain to cry out that love was only eased with love, and fancy healed by no medicine but favour. Phoebus had herbs to heal all hurts but this passion, Circe had charms for all chances but for affection, and Mercury subtle reasons to refell[3] all griefs but love. Persuasions are bootless, reason lends no remedy, counsel no comfort, to such whom fancy hath made resolute, and therefore, though Phoebe loves Ganymede, yet Montanus must honour none but Phoebe.'

---

1.   Apis Indica] The bee of India.
2.   Bellerophon] Greek myth; ancient Corinthian hero; carried a letter requesting his own execution.
3.   refell] Refute.

'Then,' quoth Ganymede, 'may I rightly term thee a despairing lover, that livest without joy and lovest without hope. But what shall I do, Montanus, to pleasure thee? Shall I despise Phoebe as she disdains thee?' 'Oh,' quoth Montanus, 'that were to renew my griefs and double my sorrows, for the sight of her discontent were the censure of my death. Alas Ganymede, though I perish in my thoughts, let not her die in her desires. Of all passions love is most impatient, then let not so fair a creature as Phoebe sink under the burden of so deep a distress. Being lovesick, she is proved heartsick, and all for the beauty of Ganymede. Thy proportion hath entangled her affection, and she is snared in the beauty of thy excellence. Then sith she loves thee so dear, mislike not her deadly. Be thou paramour to such a paragon, she hath beauty to content thine eye, and flocks to enrich thy store. Thou canst not wish for more than thou shalt win by her, for she is beautiful, virtuous and wealthy, three deep persuasions to make love frolic.' Aliena seeing Montanus cut it against the hair and plead that Ganymede ought to love Phoebe when his only life was the love of Phoebe, answered him thus: 'Why, Montanus, dost thou further this motion, seeing if Ganymede marry Phoebe thy market is clean marred?' 'Ah mistress,' quoth he, 'so hath love taught me to honour Phoebe that I would prejudice my life to pleasure her, and die in despair rather than she should perish for want. It shall suffice me to see her contented,[1] and to feed mine eye on her favour. If she marry, though it be my martyrdom, yet if she be pleased I will brook it with patience, and triumph in mine own stars to see her desires satisfied. Therefore if Ganymede be as courteous as he is beautiful, let him show his virtues in redressing Phoebe's miseries.' And this Montanus pronounced with such an assured countenance that it amazed both Aliena and Ganymede to see the resolution of his loves, so that they pitied his passions and commended his patience, devising how they might by any subtlety get Montanus the favour of Phoebe. Straight (as women's heads are full of wiles) Ganymede had a fetch to force Phoebe to fancy the shepherd, malgrado[2] the resolution of her mind; he prosecuted his policy thus: 'Montanus,' quoth he, 'seeing Phoebe is so forlorn, lest I might be counted unkind in not salving so fair a creature, I will go with thee to Phoebe and there hear herself in word utter that which she hath discoursed with her pen, and then, as love wills me, I will set down my censure. I will home by our house and send Corydon to accompany Aliena.' Montanus seemed glad of this determination, and away they go towards the house of Phoebe. When they drew nigh to the cottage, Montanus ran afore and went in and told Phoebe that Ganymede

---

1. her contented] Q2's correction: 'him' in Q1.
2. malgrado] Despite.

was at the door. This word 'Ganymede' sounding in the ears of Phoebe drove her into such an ecstasy for joy that, rising up in her bed, she was half revived, and her wan colour began to wax red; and with that came Ganymede in, who saluted Phoebe with such a courteous look that it was half a salve to her sorrows. Sitting him down by her bedside he questioned about her disease, and where the pain chiefly held her? Phoebe looking as lovely as Venus in her night-gear, tainting her face with as ruddy a blush as Clytia[1] did when she bewrayed her loves to Phoebus, taking Ganymede by the hand began thus: 'Fair shepherd, if love were not more strong then nature, or fancy the sharpest extreme, my immodesty were the more and my virtues the less, for nature hath framed women's eyes bashful, their hearts full of fear, and their tongues full of silence. But Love, that imperious Love, where his power is predominant then he perverts all and wresteth the wealth of nature to his own will: an instance in myself, fair Ganymede, for such a fire hath he kindled in my thoughts that to find ease for the flame, I was forced to pass the bounds of modesty and seek a salve at thy hands for my secret harms. Blame me not if I be overbold, for it is thy beauty, and if I be too forward it is fancy and the deep insight into thy virtues that makes me thus fond. For let me say in a word what may be contained in a volume: Phoebe loves Ganymede.' At this she held down her head and wept, and Ganymede rose as one that would suffer no fish to hang on his fingers,[2] made this reply: 'Water not thy plants, Phoebe, for I do pity thy plaints, nor seek not to discover thy loves in tears for I conjecture thy truth by thy passions; sorrow is no salve for loves, nor sighs no remedy for affection. Therefore frolic, Phoebe, for if Ganymede can cure thee, doubt not of recovery. Yet this let me say without offence, that it grieves me to thwart Montanus in his fancies, seeing his desires have been so resolute and his thoughts so loyal; but thou allegest that thou art forced from him by fate, so I tell thee Phoebe, either some star or else some destiny fits my mind rather with Adonis to die in chase than be counted a wanton on[3] Venus' knee. Although I pity thy martyrdom, yet I can grant no marriage, for though I held thee fair, yet mine eye is not fettered. Love grows not like the herb Spattana to his perfection in one night, but creeps with the snail, and yet at last attains to the top.[4] *Festina lente*,[5] especially in love, for momentary fancies are ofttimes the fruits of follies. If, Phoebe, I should like thee as the Hyperborei do their dates, which banquet with

---

1. Clytia] Girl loved by Phoebus in Ovid's *Metamorphoses*.
2. suffer … fingers] Refuse all encumbrance.
3. on] Q3's correction of Q1-2's 'in'.
4. top] Word missing in Quartos, supplied by Greg.
5. *Festina lente*] Latin: hasten slowly.

them in the morning and throw them away at night, my folly should be great and thy repentance more. Therefore I will have time to turn my thoughts, and my loves shall grow up as the watercresses, slowly but with a deep root. Thus Phoebe thou mayst see, I disdain not though I desire not, remaining indifferent till time and love makes me resolute. Therefore, Phoebe, seek not to suppress affection, and with the love of Montanus quench the remembrance of Ganymede. Strive thou to hate me as I seek to like of thee: and ever have the duties of Montanus in the mind, for I promise thee thou mayst have one more wealthy but not more loyal.' These words were corrosives[1] to the perplexed Phoebe, that sobbing out sighs and straining out tears she blubbered out these words:

'And shall I then have no salve of Ganymede but suspense, no hope but a doubtful hazard, no comfort, but be posted off to the will of time? Justly have the gods balanced my fortunes, who being cruel to Montanus, found Ganymede as unkind to myself, so in forcing him perish for love, I shall die myself with overmuch love.' 'I am glad,' quoth Ganymede, 'you look into your own faults and see where your shoe wrings you, measuring now the pains of Montanus by your own passions.' 'Truth,' quoth Phoebe, 'and so deeply I repent me of my frowardness toward the shepherd, that could I cease to love Ganymede, I would resolve to like Montanus.' 'What, if I can with reason persuade Phoebe to mislike of Ganymede, will she then favour Montanus?' 'When reason,' quoth she, 'doth quench that love that I owe to thee, then will I fancy him; conditionally, that if my love can be suppressed with no reason, as being without reason, Ganymede will only wed himself to Phoebe.' 'I grant it, fair shepherdess,' quoth he, 'and to feed thee with the sweetness of hope, this resolve on: I will never marry myself to woman but unto thyself.' And with that Ganymede gave Phoebe a fruitless kiss and such words of comfort that before Ganymede departed she arose out of her bed, and made him and Montanus such cheer as could be found in such a country cottage, Ganymede in the midst of their banquet rehearsing promises of either in Montanus' favour, which highly pleased the shepherd. Thus all three content, and soothed up in hope, Ganymede took his leave of his Phoebe and departed, leaving her a contented woman, and Montanus highly pleased. But poor Ganymede, who had her thoughts on her Rosader, when she called to remembrance his wounds, filled her eyes full of tears and her heart full of sorrows, plodded to find Aliena at the folds, thinking with her presence to drive away her passions. As she came on the plains, she might espy where Rosader and Saladyn sat with Aliena under the shade, which sight was a salve to her grief, and such a cordial unto her heart that she tripped alongst the lawns full of joy.

---

1. corrosives] Caustics for a wound.

At last Corydon, who was with them, spied Ganymede, and with that the clown rose, and running to meet him cried: 'O sirrah, a match, a match! Our mistress shall be married on Sunday.' Thus the poor peasant frolicked it before Ganymede, who coming to the crew saluted them all, and especially Rosader, saying that he was glad to see him so well recovered of his wounds. 'I had not gone abroad so soon,' quoth Rosader, 'but that I am bidden to a marriage, which on Sunday next must be solemnised between my brother and Aliena. I see well where love leads delay is loathsome, and that small wooing serves where both the parties are willing.' 'Truth,' quoth Ganymede, 'but a happy day should it be if Rosader that day might be married to Rosalynd.' 'Ah good Ganymede,' quoth he, 'by naming Rosalynd renew not my sorrows, for the thought of her perfections is the thrall of my miseries.' 'Tush, be of good cheer, man,' quoth Ganymede: 'I have a friend that is deeply experienced in necromancy and magic; what art can do shall be acted for thine advantage. I will cause him to bring in Rosalynd, if either France or any bordering nation harbour her, and upon that take the faith of a young shepherd.' Aliena smiled to see how Rosader frowned, thinking that Ganymede had jested with him. But breaking off from those matters, the page, somewhat pleasant, began to discourse unto them what had passed between him and Phoebe; which as they laughed, so they wondered at, all confessing that there is none so chaste but love will change. Thus they passed away the day in chat, and when the sun began to set they took their leaves and departed, Aliena providing for their marriage day such solemn cheer and handsome robes as fitted their country estate, and yet somewhat the better in that Rosader had promised to bring Gerismond thither as a guest. Ganymede, who then meant to discover herself before her father, had made her a gown of green, and a kirtle [1] of the finest sendal,[2] in such sort that she seemed some heavenly nymph harboured in country attire.

Saladyn was not behind in care to set out the nuptials, nor Rosader mindful to bid guests, who invited Gerismond and all his followers to the feast, who willingly granted, so that there was nothing but the day wanting to this marriage. In the meanwhile, Phoebe being a bidden guest made herself as gorgeous as might be to please the eye of Ganymede, and Montanus suited himself with the cost of many of his flocks to be gallant against that day, for then was Ganymede to give Phoebe an answer of her loves, and Montanus either to hear the doom of his misery, or the censure of his happiness. But while this gear was a-brewing, Phoebe passed not one day without visiting her Ganymede, so far was she wrapped in the beauties

---

1. kirtle] The outer petticoat of a woman's gown.
2. sendal] A thin, rich, silken material.

of this lovely swain. Much prattle they had, and the discourse of many passions, Phoebe wishing for the day, as she thought, of her welfare, and Ganymede smiling to think what unexpected events would fall out at the wedding. In these humours the week went away, that at last Sunday came.

No sooner did Phoebus' henchman appear in the sky to give warning that his master's horses should be trapped in his glorious coach, but Corydon in his holiday suit, marvellous seemly in a russet jacket welted with the same and faced with red worsted, having a pair of blue chamlet[1] sleeves bound at the wrists with four yellow laces, closed afore very richly with a dozen pewter buttons; his hose was of grey kersey[2] with a large slop[3] barred overthwart the pocket-holes with three fair guards stitched of either side with red thread; his stock was of the own, sewed close to his breech, and for to beautify his hose, he had trussed himself round with a dozen of new-threaden points of medley colour;[4] his bonnet was green, whereon stood a copper brooch with the picture of Saint Denis; and to want nothing that might make him amorous in his old days, he had a fair shirt-band of fine lockram,[5] whipped over with Coventry blue of no small cost.

Thus attired, Corydon bestirred himself as chief stickler[6] in these actions, and had strewed all the house with flowers that it seemed rather some of Flora's choice bowers than any country cottage.

Thither repaired Phoebe with all the maids of the forest, to set out the bride in the most seemliest sort that might be; but howsoever she helped to prank out[7] Aliena, yet her eye was still on Ganymede, who was so neat in a suit of grey that he seemed Endymion[8] when he won Luna with his looks, or Paris when he played the swain to get the beauty of the nymph Oenone. Ganymede, like a pretty page, waited on his mistress Aliena and overlooked that all was in a readiness against the bridegroom should come; who, attired in a forester's suit, came accompanied with Gerismond and his brother Rosader early in the morning; where arrived, they were solemnly entertained by Aliena and the rest of the country swains, Gerismond very highly commending the fortunate choice of Saladyn, in that had chosen a shepherdess whose virtues appeared in her outward beauties, being no less fair than seeming modest.

---

1.   chamlet] Camlet, rich stuff of silk and wool.   2.   kersey] Coarse cloth.
3.   slop] Loose breeches.   4.   medley colour] Mixed colour.
5.   lockram] A linen fabric.   6.   stickler] Manager.
7.   prank out] To prank; to dress or decorate showily; to make an ostentatious display.
8.   Endymion] Greek myth; a beautiful young man, famed for his eternal sleep on Mount Latmos; he was especially loved by Selene (moon).

Ganymede coming in and seeing her father began to blush, Nature working affects by her secret effects. Scarce could she abstain from tears to see her father in so low fortunes, he that was wont to sit in his royal palace, attended on by twelve noble peers, now to be contented with a simple cottage, and a troop of revelling woodmen for his train. The consideration of his fall made Ganymede full of sorrows, yet that she might triumph over Fortune with patience, and not any way dash that merry day with her dumps, she smothered her melancholy with a shadow of mirth and very reverently welcomed the king, not according to his former degree, but to his present estate, with such diligence as Gerismond began to commend the page for his exquisite person and excellent qualities.

As thus the king with his foresters frolicked it among the shepherds, Corydon came in with a fair mazer full of cider, and presented it to Gerismond with such a clownish salute that he began to smile and took it of the old shepherd very kindly, drinking to Aliena and the rest of her fair maids, amongst whom Phoebe was the foremost. Aliena pledged the king and drunk to Rosader, so the carouse went round from him to Phoebe, etc. As they were thus drinking and ready to go to church, came in Montanus, apparelled all in tawny to signify that he was forsaken. On his head he wore a garland of willow, his bottle hanged by his side, whereon was painted despair, and on his sheephook hung two sonnets as labels of his loves and fortunes.

Thus attired came Montanus in, with his face as full of grief as his heart was of sorrows, showing in his countenance the map of extremities. As soon as the shepherds saw him, they did him all the honour they could, as being the flower of all the swains in Arden, for a bonnier boy was there not seen since the wanton wag of Troy[1] that kept sheep in Ida.[2] He, seeing the king, and guessing it to be Gerismond, did him all the reverence his country courtesy could afford, insomuch that the king, wondering at his attire, began to question what he was. Montanus overhearing him made this reply:

'I am, sir,' quoth he, 'Love's swain, as full of inward discontents as I seem fraught with outward follies. Mine eyes like bees delight in sweet flowers, but sucking their full on the fair of beauty, they carry home to the hive of my heart far more gall than honey, and for one drop of pure dew, a ton full of deadly aconiton. I hunt with the fly to pursue the eagle, that flying too nigh the sun, I perish with the sun. My thoughts are above my reach, and my desires more than my fortunes, yet neither greater than my loves.

---

1. wag of Troy] Paris.
2. Ida] Range of mountains in southern Phrygia. It was here that the Trojan Paris was said to have been exposed and brought up by shepherds.

But daring with Phaethon, I fall with Icarus, and seeking to pass the mean, I die for being so mean. My night-sleeps are waking slumbers, as full of sorrows as they be far from rest, and my days' labours are fruitless amours, staring at a star and stumbling at a straw, leaving reason to follow after repentance. Yet every passion is a pleasure though it pinch, because love hides his wormseed[1] in figs, his poisons in sweet potions, and shadows prejudice with the mask of pleasure. The wisest counsellors are my deep discontents, and I hate that which should salve my harm, like the patient which stung with the tarantula loathes music, and yet the disease incurable but by melody. Thus, sir, restless I hold myself remediless, as loving without either reward or regard, and yet loving because there is none worthy to be loved but the mistress of my thoughts. And that I am as full of passions as I have discoursed in my plaints, sir, if you please, see my sonnets, and by them censure of my sorrows.'

These words of Montanus brought the king into a great wonder, amazed as much at his wit as his attire, insomuch that he took the papers off his hook and read them to this effect:

Montanus' first Sonnet.

Alas! how wander I amidst these woods,
Whereas no day-bright shine doth find access;
But where the melancholy fleeting floods,
Dark as the night, my night of woes express.
Disarmed of reason, spoiled of nature's goods,
Without redress to salve my heaviness
    I walk, whilst thought, too cruel to my harms,
    With endless grief my heedless judgement charms.

My silent tongue assailed by secret fear,
My traitorous eyes imprisoned in their joy,
My fatal peace devoured in feigned cheer,
My heart enforced to harbour in annoy,
My reason robbed of power by yielding ear,
My fond opinions slave to every toy.
    O Love! thou guide in my uncertain way,
    Woe to thy bow, thy fire, the cause of my decay.

Et florida pungunt.[2]

---

1. wormseed] Probably variant of 'wormwood', associated with bitterness.
2. *Et florida pungunt*] Latin: Even flowers sting. See p. 105 n. 1.

When the king had read this sonnet, he highly commended the device of the shepherd that could so wittily wrap his passions in a shadow, and so covertly conceal that which bred his chiefest discontent, affirming, that as the least shrubs have their tops, the smallest hairs their shadows, so the meanest swains had their fancies, and in their kind were as chary of love as a king. Whetted on with this device, he took the second and read it. The effects were these:

Montanus' second Sonnet.

When the dog
Full of rage,
    With his ireful eyes
    Frowns amidst the skies,
The shepherd to assuage
    The fury of the heat,
    Himself doth safely seat

By a fount
Full of fair,
    Where a gentle breath,
    Mounting from beneath,
Tempereth the air.

There his flocks
Drink their fill,
    And with ease repose,
    Whilst sweet sleep doth close
Eyes from toilsome ill.

But I burn
Without rest,
    No defensive power
    Shields from Phoebe's lour:
Sorrow is my best.
Gentle Love,
Lour no more,
    If thou wilt invade,
    In the secret shade,
Labour not so sore.

I myself
And my flocks
    They their love to please,
    I myself to ease,

> Both leave the shady oaks:
> Content to burn in fire
> Sith Love doth so desire.

Et florida pungunt.

Gerismond, seeing the pithy vein of those sonnets, began to make further enquiry what he was. Whereupon Rosader discoursed unto him the love of Montanus to Phoebe, his great loyalty and her deep cruelty, and how in revenge the gods had made the curious nymph amorous of young Ganymede. Upon this discourse, the king was desirous to see Phoebe, who being brought before Gerismond by Rosader, shadowed the beauty of her face with such a vermilion teinture that the king's eyes began to dazzle at the purity of her excellence. After Gerismond had fed his looks awhile upon her fair, he questioned with her why she rewarded Montanus' love with so little regard, seeing his deserts were many, and his passions extreme. Phoebe to make a reply to the king's demand, answered thus: 'Love, sir, is chary in his laws, and whatsoever he sets down for justice, be it never so unjust, the sentence cannot be reversed. Women's fancies lend favours not ever by desert, but as they are enforced by their desires, for fancy is tied to the wings of Fate, and what the stars decree stands for an infallible doom. I know Montanus is wise, and women's ears are greatly delighted with wit, as hardly escaping the charm of a pleasant tongue, as Ulysses the melody of the Sirens. Montanus is beautiful, and women's eyes are snared in the excellence of objects, as desirous to feed their looks with a fair face, as the bee to suck on a sweet flower. Montanus is wealthy, and an ounce of *give me* persuades a woman more than a pound of *hear me*. Danae was won with a golden shower when she could not be gotten with all the entreats of Jupiter. I tell you sir, the string of a woman's heart reacheth to the pulse of her hand, and let a man rub that with gold, and 'tis hard but she will prove his heart's gold. Montanus is young, a great clause in fancy's court; Montanus is virtuous, the richest argument that love yields; and yet knowing all these perfections, I praise them and wonder at them, loving the qualities, but not affecting the person, because the Destinies have set down a contrary censure. Yet Venus, to add revenge, hath given me wine of the same grape, a sip of the same sauce, and firing me with the like passion, hath crossed me with as ill a penance, for I am in love with a shepherd's swain, as coy to me as I am cruel to Montanus, as peremptory in disdain as I was perverse in desire – and that is,' quoth she, 'Aliena's page, young Ganymede.'

Gerismond, desirous to prosecute the end of these passions, called in Ganymede, who, knowing the case, came in graced with such a blush as beautified the crystal of his face with a ruddy brightness. The king noting well the physiognomy of Ganymede, began by his favours to call to mind the face of his Rosalynd, and with that fetched a deep sigh. Rosader, that was passing familiar with Gerismond, demanded of him why he sighed so sore. 'Because Rosader,' quoth he, 'the favour of Ganymede puts me in mind of Rosalynd.' At this word Rosader sighed so deeply as though his heart would have burst. 'And what's the matter,' quoth Gerismond, 'that you quite me with such a sigh?' 'Pardon me, sir,' quoth Rosader, 'because I love none but Rosalynd.' 'And upon that condition,' quoth Gerismond, 'that Rosalynd were here, I would this day make up a marriage betwixt her and thee.' At this Aliena turned her head and smiled upon Ganymede, and she could scarce keep countenance. Yet she salved all with secrecy, and Gerismond to drive away such dumps, questioned with Ganymede what the reason was he regarded not Phoebe's love, seeing she was as fair as the wanton that brought Troy to ruin. Ganymede mildly answered: 'If I should affect the fair Phoebe, I should offer poor Montanus great wrong, to win that from him in a moment that he hath laboured for so many months. Yet have I promised to the beautiful shepherdess to wed myself never to woman except unto her, but with this promise, that if I can by reason suppress Phoebe's love towards me, she shall like of none but of Montanus.' 'To that,' quoth Phoebe, 'I stand, for my love is so far beyond reason as it will admit no persuasion of reason.' 'For justice,' quoth he, 'I appeal to Gerismond.' 'And to his censure will I stand,' quoth Phoebe. 'And in your victory,' quoth Montanus, 'stands the hazard of my fortunes, for if Ganymede go away with conquest, Montanus is in conceit love's monarch; if Phoebe win, then am I in effect most miserable.' 'We will see this controversy,' quoth Gerismond, 'and then we will to church: therefore, Ganymede, let us hear your argument.' 'Nay, pardon my absence awhile,' quoth she, 'and you shall see one in store.' In went Ganymede and dressed herself in woman's attire, having on a gown of green, with kirtle of rich sendal, so quaint that she seemed Diana triumphing in the forest. Upon her head she wore a chaplet of roses, which gave her such a grace that she looked like Flora perked in the pride of all her flowers. Thus attired came Rosalynd in, and presented herself at her father's feet, with her eyes full of tears, craving his blessing, and discoursing unto him all her fortunes, how she was banished by Torismond, and how ever since she lived in that country disguised.

Gerismond, seeing his daughter, rose from his seat and fell upon her neck, uttering the passions of his joy in watery plaints, driven into such an ecstasy of content that he could not utter one word. At this sight, if Rosader was both amazed and joyful, I refer myself to the judgement of such as have experience in love, seeing his Rosalynd before his face whom so long and deeply he had affected. At last Gerismond recovered his spirits and in most fatherly terms entertained his daughter Rosalynd, after many questions demanding of her what had passed between her and Rosader. 'So much, sir,' quoth she, 'as there wants nothing but your grace to make up the marriage.' 'Why then,' quoth Gerismond, 'Rosader take her, she is thine, and let this day solemnise both thy brother's and thy nuptials.' Rosader beyond measure content, humbly thanked the king and embraced his Rosalynd, who turning towards Phoebe demanded if she had shown sufficient reason to suppress the force of her loves. 'Yea,' quoth Phoebe, 'and so great a persuasive, that please it you, madam, and Aliena, to give us leave, Montanus and I will make this day the third couple in marriage.' She had no sooner spoke this word, but Montanus threw away his garland of willow, his bottle where was painted despair, and cast his sonnets in the fire, showing himself as frolic as Paris when he handselled[1] his love with Helena. At this Gerismond and the rest smiled, and concluded that Montanus and Phoebe should keep their wedding with the two brethren. Aliena seeing Saladyn stand in a dump, to wake him from his dream began thus: 'Why, how now, my Saladyn, all amort? What melancholy, man, at the day of marriage? Perchance thou art sorrowful to think on thy brother's high fortunes, and thine own base desires to choose so mean a shepherdess? Cheer up thy heart, man, for this day thou shalt be married to the daughter of a king: for know, Saladyn, I am not Aliena, but Alinda, the daughter of thy mortal enemy Torismond.'

At this all the company was amazed, especially Gerismond, who rising up, took Alinda in his arms, and said to Rosalynd: 'Is this that fair Alinda, famous for so many virtues, that forsook her father's court to live with thee exiled in the country?' 'The same,' quoth Rosalynd. 'Then,' quoth Gerismond, turning to Saladyn, 'jolly forester be frolic, for thy fortunes are great, and thy desires excellent. Thou hast got a princess as famous for her perfection as exceeding in proportion.' 'And she hath with her beauty won,' quoth Saladyn, 'an humble servant as full of faith as she of amiable favour.' While everyone was amazed with these comical[2] events, Corydon came skipping in and told them that the priest was at church and tarried for their coming. With that, Gerismond led the way and the rest followed, where to the admiration of all the country swains in Arden, their marriages were solemnly solemnized. As soon as the priest had finished, home they went with Alinda, where Corydon had made all things in readiness. Dinner was provided, and the tables being spread, and the brides set down by Gerismond, Rosader, Saladyn and Montanus that day were servitors. Homely cheer they had, such as their country could afford, but to mend their fare they had mickle good chat and many discourses of their

---

1. handselled] Sealed.   2. comical] Fortunate, happy.

loves and fortunes. About mid-dinner, to make them merry, Corydon came in with an old crowd[1] and played them a fit of mirth, to which he sung this pleasant song:

Corydon's Song.

A blithe and bonny country lass,
    heigh ho, the bonny lass!
Sat sighing on the tender grass
    and weeping said, 'Will none come woo me?'
A smicker[2] boy, a lither[3] swain,
    heigh ho, a smicker swain!
That in his love was wanton fain,
    with smiling looks straight came unto her.

Whenas the wanton wench espied,
    heigh ho, when she espied!
The means to make herself a bride,
    she simpered smooth like Bonnybell:[4]
The swain that saw her squint-eyed kind,
    heigh ho, so squint-eyed kind!
His arms about her body twined
    and said, 'Fair lass, how fare ye, well?'

The country kit said: 'Well, forsooth,
    heigh ho, well forsooth!
But that I have a longing tooth,
    a longing tooth that makes me cry.'
'Alas!' said he, 'what gars[5] thy grief?
    heigh ho, what garres thy grief?'
'A wound,' quoth she, 'without relief,
    I fear a maid that I shall die.'

'If that be all,' the shepherd said,
    heigh ho, the shepherd said!
'I'll make thee wive it, gentle maid,
    And so recure thy malady.'

---

1. crowd] A stringed instrument.
2. smicker] Smart.
3. lither] Nimble.
4. Bonnybell] Name from ballad in Spenser's *Shepheardes Calender* (August), which Corydon's song imitates.
5. gars] Causes.

Hereon they kissed with many a oath,
    heigh ho, with many a oath!
And 'fore god Pan did plight their troth,
    and to the church they hied them fast.

And God send every pretty peat,
    heigh ho, the pretty peat![1]
That fears to die of this conceit,
    so kind a friend to help at last.

Corydon having thus made them merry, as they were in the midst of all their jollity, word was brought in to Saladyn and Rosader that a brother of theirs, one Fernandyn, was arrived, and desired to speak with them. Gerismond overhearing this news, demanded who it was. 'It is, sir,' quoth Rosader, 'our middle brother, that lives a scholar in Paris; but what fortune hath driven him to seek us out I know not.' With that Saladyn went and met his brother, whom he welcomed with all courtesy, and Rosader gave him no less friendly entertainment. Brought he was by his two brothers into the parlour where they all sat at dinner. Fernandyn, as one that knew as many manners as he could points of sophistry, and was as well brought up as well lettered, saluted them all. But when he espied Gerismond, kneeling on his knee he did him what reverence belonged to his estate, and with that burst forth into these speeches: 'Although, right mighty prince, this day of my brothers' marriage be a day of mirth, yet time craves another course, and therefore from dainty cates rise to sharp weapons. And you, the sons of Sir John of Bordeaux, leave off your amours and fall to arms; change your loves into lances, and now this day show yourselves as valiant as hitherto you have been passionate. For know, Gerismond, that hard by at the edge of this forest the twelve peers of France are up in arms to recover thy right, and Torismond, trooped with a crew of desperate renegades, is ready to bid them battle. The armies are ready to join, therefore show thyself in the field to encourage thy subjects, and you, Saladyn and Rosader, mount you, and show yourselves as hardy soldiers as you have been hearty lovers, so shall you for the benefit of your country discover the idea of your father's virtues to be stamped in your thoughts, and prove children worthy of so honourable a parent.' At this alarum given by Fernandyn, Gerismond leapt from the board, and Saladyn and Rosader betook themselves to their weapons. 'Nay,' quoth Gerismond, 'go with me, I have horse and armour for us all, and then being well mounted, let us show that we can carry revenge and honour at our falchions'[2] points.'

---

1.   peat] Girl.
2.   falchions] Swords.

Thus they leave the brides full of sorrow, especially Alinda, who desired Gerismond to be good to her father. He, not returning a word because his haste was great, hied him home to his lodge, where he delivered Saladyn and Rosader horse and armour, and himself armed royally led the way, not having ridden two leagues before they discovered where in a valley both the battles were joined. Gerismond seeing the wing wherein the peers fought, thrust in there and cried 'Saint Denis!' Gerismond laying on such load upon his enemies that he showed how highly he did estimate of a crown. When the peers perceived that their lawful king was there, they grew more eager; and Saladyn and Rosader so behaved themselves that none durst stand in their way, nor abide the fury of their weapons. To be short, the peers were conquerors, Torismond's army put to flight, and himself slain in battle. The peers then gathered themselves together, and saluting their king, conducted him royally into Paris, where he was received with great joy of all the citizens. As soon as all was quiet and he had received again the crown, he sent for Alinda and Rosalynd to the court, Alinda being very passionate[1] for the death of her father, yet brooking it with the more patience in that she was contented with the welfare of her Saladyn. Well, as soon as they were come to Paris, Gerismond made a royal feast for the peers and lords of his land, which continued thirty days, in which time summoning a parliament, by the consent of his nobles he created Rosader heir-apparent to the kingdom, he restored Saladyn to all his father's land, and gave him the Dukedom of Nameurs, he made Fernandyn principal secretary to himself, and that fortune might every way seem frolic, he made Montanus lord over all the forest of Arden, Adam Spencer captain of the king's guard, and Corydon master of Alinda's flocks.

Here, gentlemen, may you see in Euphues' Golden Legacy, that such as neglect their fathers' precepts incur much prejudice; that division in nature, as it is a blemish in nurture, so 'tis a breach of good fortunes; that virtue is not measured by birth but by action; that younger brethren, though inferior in years, yet may be superior to honours; that concord is the sweetest conclusion, and amity betwixt brothers more forceable than fortune. If you gather any fruits by this legacy, speak well of Euphues for writing it, and me for fetching it. If you grace me with that favour, you encourage me to be more forward, and as soon as I have overlooked my labours, expect the Sailor's Calendar.[2]

T. Lodge.

FINIS.

---

1. passionate] Sorrowful.
2. Sailor's Calendar] Another of Lodge's works, now lost.

Bibliography

The most accurate old-spelling text of *Rosalynd* is that in *A New Variorum Edition of Shakespeare: As You Like It*, edited by Richard Knowles (New York, 1977), to which we are much indebted. W. W. Greg's modern-spelling edition, cited in note 1 to the introduction, has useful textual notes but many inaccuracies. Lodge's complete works were edited by Edmund Gosse for the Hunterian Club in 4 vols. (1875–83, repr. New York, 1963).

Biographies: Elaine Cuvelier, *Thomas Lodge: Témoin de son temps (c. 1558–1625)* (Collection Etudes Anglaises 85; Paris, 1984); W. D. Rae, *Thomas Lodge* (New York, 1967); M. Ryan, Jr, *Thomas Lodge, Gentleman* (Hamden, Conn., 1959); C. J. Sisson, *Lodge and Other Elizabethans* (Cambridge, Mass., 1933); E. A. Tenney, *Thomas Lodge* (Ithaca, NY, 1935).

General critical works on Elizabethan prose fiction: Walter R. Davis, *Idea and Act in Elizabethan Fiction* (Princeton, NJ, 1969); Richard Helgerson, *The Elizabethan Prodigals* (Berkeley, Calif., 1976); Arthur F. Kinney, *Humanist Poetics* (Amherst, 1986); C. S. Lewis, *English Literature in the Sixteenth Century Excluding Drama* (Oxford, 1954); David Margolies, *Novel and Society in Elizabethan England* (London, 1985); William Nelson, *Fact or Fiction: The Dilemma of the Renaissance Storyteller* (Cambridge, Mass., 1973); Paul Salzman, *English Prose Fiction 1558–1700* (Oxford, 1985).

***Rosalynd* as source for *As You Like It*:** editions by Knowles (pp. 475–83) and Greg (pp. 187–209) cited above; Marco Mincoff, 'What Shakespeare did to *Rosalynde*', *Shakespeare Jahrbuch* 96 (1960), 78–89; Geoffrey Bullough, in *Narrative and Dramatic Sources of Shakespeare*, vol.2 (London, 1958), pp.145–55; Hallett Smith, *Shakespeare's Romances* (San Marino, Calif., 1972), pp. 71–94.

Gender in *Rosalynd*: Janice Paran, 'The Amorous Girl-Boy: Sexual Ambiguity in Thomas Lodge's *Rosalynde*', *Assays* 1 (1981), 91–7; Louise Schleiner, 'Ladies and Gentlemen in Two Genres of Elizabethan Prose Fiction', *Studies in English Literature* 29 (1989), 1–20.

RYBURN RENAISSANCE TEXTS AND STUDIES
produced in association with
Northern Renaissance Seminar Text Group

Other titles include

The Tragedy of Mariam, the Fair Queen of Jewry
by Elizabeth Cary
Edited by Stephanie J. Wright

Jacobean Civic Pageants
Edited by Richard Dutton